Spirituality
& Social Action

Spirituality
& Social Action

ANDY HARRIS

WIPF & STOCK · Eugene, Oregon

SPIRITUALITY & SOCIAL ACTION

Wipf & Stock
An Imprint of Wipf and Stock Publishers
199 W. 8th Ave., Suite 3
Eugene, OR 97401

www.wipfandstock.com

PAPERBACK ISBN: 978-1-7252-6346-8
HARDCOVER ISBN: 978-1-7252-6347-5
EBOOK ISBN: 978-1-7252-6348-2

Manufactured in the U.S.A.   04/07/20

To my spiritual mentors for their profound influence on my faith and for being the inspiration for this book: my parents—Irving and Julie Harris, William Sloane Coffin, Gert Behanna, Marge Lottis, Brennan Manning, Richard Rohr, Ched Myers, Barry Heath, Chris Haydon, and my daughter, Jennifer Harris Morris, missionary in Peru since 1997.

He gives strength to the weary and increases the power of the weak.
Even youths grow tired and weary, and young men stumble and fall;
But those who hope in the Lord will renew their strength.
They will soar on wings like eagles;
They will run and not grow weary, they will walk and not be faint.

—ISAIAH 40:29–31

Then you will call upon me and come and pray to me, and I will
listen to you. You will seek me and find me when you seek me with
all your heart.

—JEREMIAH 29:12–13

You trample on the poor and force him to give you grain. Therefore,
though you have built stone mansions, you will not live in them;
though you have planted lush vineyards, you will not drink their wine.
For I know how many are your offenses and how great your sins.

—AMOS 5:11

And what does the Lord require of you? To act justly and love mercy
and to walk humbly with your God.

—MICAH 6:8

This is what the Lord Almighty says: "Administer true justice, show
mercy and compassion to one another. Do not oppress the widow or
the fatherless, the alien or the poor. In your hearts do not think evil
of each other."

—ZECHARIAH 7:12

Contents

Acknowledgement

I GRATEFULLY ACKNOWLEDGE THE advice and editing of Lou Masson, author and emeritus professor of English at the University of Portland.

Introduction

OUR PLANET AND THE people who inhabit it are experiencing un-precedented stress and turmoil. In these fraught times, *Spirituality & Social Action* takes a deep dive into how to move forward through a spiritual awakening and a commitment to social, economic, and racial justice. Through the process of connecting with God, we can more effectively reach out to others with love and compassion.

Pastor Daniel Hill writes, "A spiritual rebirth ushers in both the salvation of our souls and our participation in the redemption of this world. It is also to hold together activism and evangelism; protest and prayer; personal piety and social justice; intimacy with Jesus and proximity to the poor."[1]

If you, like so many others, have put thoughts and concerns about God on the back burner of your life, it may be time to bring the saucepan forward and stir in some fresh ingredients. Humans are doing a poor job of managing the planet and responding to the needs of our coinhabitants. It's time to seek God's direction, and with renewed faith, to serve our brothers and sisters next door, in our communities, and around the world. This book aims to raise consciousness about spirituality and social justice, allowing us to move forward with conviction and hope.

Here are a few practical tips to navigate your way through this book:

1. Hill, *White Awake*, 144.

- God is not referred to with a pronoun denoting gender, except when I quote some other source. I believe God is not restricted by gender.

- I have tried to avoid Christian jargon and clichés, as they sound exclusive and are often offensive to non-Christians.

- I generally don't use the title "Saint" before Paul or anyone else, as this is a concept of organized religion.

- The New International Version translation of the Bible is used exclusively, unless otherwise noted.

- Books of the Bible are spelled out in their entirety, not abbreviated, to make them more recognizable to readers who rarely frequent the Bible.

Andy Harris, April 5, 2020

CHAPTER 1

In the Pressure Cooker

IN THESE FRAUGHT TIMES, we the people have had enough. We have had enough of mass shootings of innocent civilians, including school children. Enough of political polarization, divisive language, and legislative gridlock. Enough of racism, racial injustice, and white supremacy. Enough of refugees dying in leaky boats in the Mediterranean, and children separated from parents in detention facilities on the US-Mexico border. Enough of increasing economic disparity between rich and poor. Enough of toxic pollutants poisoning children, killing off bees, and polluting our rivers, land, skies, and seas. Enough of increasing suicide rates, epidemic drug addiction, widespread homelessness, and high incarceration rates, especially for African-Americans. Enough of leaders ignoring climate disruption and the specter of nuclear weapons, both of which threaten life on Earth.

We have hoped that political institutions would save us, but they haven't. We have sought out gurus to lead us through the wilderness, but little seems to change. We have joined support groups of all types, and yet the existential crises press us from all sides. We feel frustrated, disempowered, and depressed. No wonder so many people take anti-depressants, and some people choose to ignore the news altogether. We feel like we live in a pressure cooker of a society, and the temperature just keeps getting hotter.

For many people God seems distant and aloof, a nonparticipant in our time of crisis. On social media sites people identify themselves as "spiritual but not religious," or as agnostics or atheists, who have given up altogether on God and religious institutions. With some exceptions, church attendance is on the decline because organized religion seems irrelevant, especially to the younger generation. In Portland, Oregon, my hometown, only about 18% of residents regularly attend churches, synagogues, mosques, or temples. Restaurants serving Sunday brunch have lines that snake down the block, while church pews sit half-empty on Sunday mornings. We suffer from a spiritual crisis, and many see little hope to reconnect with a God who seems detached and indifferent.

And yet, what if God does care about this dysfunctional world, a God who loves us and is trying to connect with us? As worries overwhelm us, many of us have become so distracted by our busy lives that we have little time or interest to explore a spiritual dimension. When we drive, we often listen to news or music on the radio, and when we walk or jog, we plug into our favorite music playlist or listen to audiobooks. Advertisements, text messages, emails, tweets, and even robocalls barrage us constantly. Who wouldn't feel overwhelmed in a society where the pace of life increases with each passing year? Why would we want to introduce one more thing into our already frenetic schedules? Spirituality? Be serious!

The younger generation, in particular, is wired to social media. An hour without their cell phone connection and most teens and twenty-somethings get distracted and twitchy, as with other addictions. What might their teen network be saying about them? Who might be dissing them? Social media often interrupts their concentration at school, while driving, at work, and while studying. Take away a teenager's cell phone and she/he is likely to respond with a tirade.

It's time to reconsider spirituality and to see if it offers answers to some of the pressing issues of our day. Brené Brown's definition of spirituality resonates with me: "Spirituality is recognizing and celebrating that we are all inextricably connected to each other by a power greater than all of us, and that our connection to that power and to one another is grounded in love and compassion."[1]

As a physician and activist, I have devoted a lifetime to healing and social justice. My inspiration comes from the teachings of Jesus, but also from the prophets, psalms, and from other religious traditions. I am convinced we cannot solve our current crises without a personal connection to God and a collective commitment to seek God's plan for the world. We need to come back into a right relationship with the sacred, with one another, and with the Earth.

The prophets lamented the greed and oppression of their day but spoke of hope for the future. Jeremiah wrote, "For surely I know the plans I have for you, says the Lord, plans for your welfare and not for harm, to give you a future with hope" (Jeremiah 29:11). God cares deeply about the world—it's God's creation after all—and about every being on the planet. God wants to be fully engaged in our lives and desires that we take an active role in bringing God's kingdom to Earth.

Many of us have been on some type of spiritual journey, however vague it may be and peripheral to our daily lives. We may have encountered some contact with religion in childhood, then dropped out, with no interest to further explore faith. Now we have jobs, family, civic responsibilities, friends, entertainment, and a host of other activities to fill our days to overflowing. We couldn't wedge faith into our schedule with a crowbar! And yet there is a nagging sense that we may have missed something significant. What if God exists? What would this mean for our lives, and how would this impact the way we see and treat others? Would this change how we relate to issues like poverty, justice, and racism?

God may reach out to us in a variety of ways, such as in the wonders of nature, in conversation with people of faith, through Scripture, books and tapes, via music and the performing arts, and through great sorrow and pain. We are likely to be more receptive to God's presence when we are able to get away from society's distractions: a walk in the woods, while contemplating a sunset, beside the lapping waves of a lake or ocean, or in the quiet of the predawn

---

1. Brown, *Gifts of Imperfection*, 64.

morning. It may even happen in a place of worship (imagine that!), or in dialogue among close friends, or during a time of crisis or personal loss, when we are vulnerable and searching for meaning.

I am convinced that God desires to have a personal and intimate relationship with each of us. When we begin to connect with God, however tenuous that may be, our frame of reference shifts from our narrow and often petty perspective to an expanded view of reconciliation and hope. Whether people have any religious affiliation, most have an innate sense of a higher power. Humans are wired to have a deep longing to connect with this creative force that we refer to as God, Creator, Yahweh, Allah, Great Spirit, or by many other titles. In ancient Jewish tradition the name for God was unspeakable.

Too often organized religion has not encouraged people to have a close, personal relationship with God, nor given them the tools to do so. When a priest serves as an intermediary between an individual and God, as in the Catholic confessional, it can be a stumbling block to experiencing God directly. The hypocrisy, self-righteousness, and scandals of some religious institutions have turned people off from organized religion. At times the church has bought into affluence, consumerism, militarism, nationalism, and discrimination on race, gender, or sexual orientation. People question the relevance of the church when it has adopted many of the same secular values of American society.

Jesus modeled a very different life of humility and powerlessness, values that seem almost un-American. The church finds itself caught between the radical teachings and sacrificial example of Jesus, which may offend some ears, and a desire to blend in with American values that have broader, popular appeal. All too often this conflict results in a lukewarm message from the pulpit that doesn't challenge a congregation to a personal spiritual encounter with God.

Since the Age of Reason many of us have gotten stuck in rational thinking, as if it were the pinnacle of human achievement. We trust only what can be proven scientifically or empirically. We are leery of a spiritual dimension that cannot be understood and proven with a rational mind. And yet we are able to move to sublime levels by great visual art, music, or the performing arts, such as Michelangelo's *David*, Handel's *Messiah*, or Tchaikovsky's *Swan Lake*. Similarly, the astounding variety and beauty of nature, such as a sunset, the sound of a lark, or the delicate beauty of wild-flowers, may catch us by surprise, take away our breath, and give us a glimpse of a spiritual dimension.

Jewish theologian Abraham Joshua Heschel wrote, "Awe enables us to perceive in the world intimations of the divine, to sense in small things the beginning of infinite significance, to sense the ultimate in the common and the simple; to feel in the rush of the passing the stillness of the eternal."[2]

We move from rational thought into our emotions when we fall in love, in the delight of human friendships, and at the birth of a baby. I was not allowed in the delivery room for the birth of my oldest daughter, but rules changed, and I enjoyed the immense wonder of being present at the birth of my younger daughter and son. Other human emotions, including grief, loss, and despair, also put us in touch with our emotional sensitivity.

Why is it such a "leap of faith" for many people to explore the spiritual dimension? To me the universe holds a rich tapestry of science, knowledge, and spirituality of which we understand and appreciate just a tiny fraction. Connecting with God is about letting go of our usual props and security. Think of the time you first learned how to ride a bike. For me, I thought my cousin was running behind me down the driveway holding onto my bike seat, but when I looked over my shoulder, I realized that I was riding the bike all by myself. What a sense of elation and pride!

A decisive moment arises in the Gospels when an intellectual asks Jesus to prioritize the commandments. "One of the teachers of the law came and heard them debating. Noticing that Jesus had given them a good answer, he asked him, 'Of all the commandments, which is the most important?' 'The most important one,' answered Jesus, 'is this: Love the Lord your God with all your heart and with all your soul and with all your mind and with all your

---

2. Heschel, *God in Search of Man*, 76.

strength. The second is this: Love your neighbor as yourself. There is no commandment greater than these'" (Mark 12:28–31).

This universal truth to love God above all else predates Jesus and is one of the major themes that run through the Old Testament. It is evident in the lives of Abraham, Moses, Samuel, David, and the prophets, among many others. Love God and the rest of life will take care of itself. When we come close to God, we cannot help but to live a life of humility, compassion, and service. What Jesus did was to demonstrate God's love, forgiveness, and compassion. "Anyone who has seen me has seen the Father" (John 14:9). Jesus did not preach a legalistic religion—in fact he railed against such falsehood—but rather he exemplified a life of communion with God and service to others.

God loves each of us, irrespective of our past, what we have done or what we have failed to do. God is omnipresent, out there in the world and also residing at the core of our being. It seems that what God desires most is to engage in a deep and ongoing relationship with each of us. Our role is to open ourselves to humbly receive God's love. We can start by asking forgiveness for all the years that we placed roadblocks between God and ourselves, including our egos, our rational minds, our busyness, and our willfulness. We need to let go of these false props.

Faith is about trusting and starting afresh. When we allow ourselves to be open to exploring the mystery of God, we are able to access this spiritual dimension through prayer and meditation. Faith is choosing to enter uncharted waters, alone and without hubris or ego. It is not rational; to the contrary it seems risky and may have unpredictable outcomes. And yet we humans have been formed in the image of the Creator, and our lives will be incomplete until we open ourselves to God's presence. God is calling us to be bearers of divine light, love, and compassion, and how that plays out is our unique spiritual journey.

CHAPTER 2

Dealing with Stress and Loss

I WAS AN OVERWORKED, slightly jaded medical student at the University of Virginia when I happened upon a three-night series on spirituality, given by Gert Behanna, a diminutive woman in her seventies. Gert was so short that we could see only the top half of her face over the lectern, but her voice had spunk and fire that belied her age and stature. I was enthralled.

Gert had been raised as the spoiled and only child of a wealthy family who lived at the Waldorf Astoria in New York City. I had never heard of anyone who had lived in a hotel all her life, much less a ritzy place like the Waldorf. Gert had found nothing meaningful in her life and had drifted into alcoholism. One day she attempted to end her miserable life by cutting her wrists. She was devastated to wake up in a hospital room, feeling like a failure both in her life and in her attempted suicide. She was not a religious person and had never cooked a day in her life, but the first two things she asked for were a Bible and *The Joy of Cooking*.

The more I listened to Gert, the more intrigued I became. When she offered to meet individually with meeting attendees, I eagerly signed up. It turned out that Gert knew my parents, Irv and Julie Harris, Christian leaders also from New York City. I had been raised in the Christian tradition, but in my youth it was my parents' faith, not my own. At college I fell away from church attendance, except to occasionally hear the compelling and fiery oratory of Yale's chaplain, William Sloane Coffin. Gert Behanna's message was the spark that ignited my faith journey, sometimes burning brightly, sometimes smoldering, and sometimes just ashes. But my soul was stirred that day, and the spark has survived success and failure, family and divorce, career and retirement.

I admit that a faith-centered life initially seemed pretty extreme to me. All too often I put God on the back burner, available in case of emergency, but not an active participant in the intense roller coaster of life. My other interests—family, work, community engagement, various nonprofits, a farm, sports, etc.—took precedence over faith and consumed all available time, and then some. But the tug of spirituality kept pulling me into its force field.

As an ophthalmologist I treated eyes traumatized by automobile crashes, foreign bodies, industrial accidents, and fireworks. I spent many hours talking about the necessity of wearing safety glasses, protective goggles, and helmets. Together with a pediatrician colleague, we lobbied legislators about the risk of eye injuries with BB guns, and the need to require manufacturers to put warning labels on BB gun packaging.

Just as our bodies are vulnerable to injuries and may become broken, so too each of us is a broken, imperfect being. We may seek the right path, but we inevitably stumble along the way. As the apostle Paul wrote, "I do not understand what I do . . . For I have the desire to do what is good, but I cannot carry it out. For what I do is not the good I want to do; no, the evil I do not want to do—this I keep on doing" (Romans 7:15, 18–19).

When I was forty-two, I was devastated one evening to learn that that my marriage was breaking apart. It was the hardest thing I had ever encountered by a long shot. I was naïve enough to think that divorce was simply not an option. But by the grace of God, two spiritual mentors promptly showed up in my life. The next morning a patient and spiritual guide, Marge Lottis, walked into my exam room, and I poured out my heart for over an hour. I seriously doubt we ever got to her eye exam! But we ended up meeting every two weeks for the next several months, and these times of sharing were a critical factor in my healing and recovery and spiritual growth.

That same weekend Brennan Manning, a laicized Franciscan priest and author of twenty-three books, including *The Ragamuffin Gospel*, led a spiritual seminar in my hometown, and I soaked up every word he spoke. When I was hurting the most, God's servants were there to guide me through the darkness with their wisdom and compassion. I felt touched by God's love and eventually came to feel hope amidst the anguish of divorce.

When everything is going well, and we are happy and self-satisfied, we have a tendency to forget about God. The Bible is full of stories of the Israelites, God's chosen people, losing their way and turning away from God, even making the image of a golden calf to worship in the wilderness. Our materialism and distractions are our own golden calves. It is unfortunate but true that we are most likely to seek God when we are suffering and feeling overwhelmed, such as the tragic loss of a loved one, a diagnosis of cancer, a job loss, drug or alcohol addiction, or whatever else brings us face to face with reality and lays bare our lives.

It was not easy for me to come through the dark tunnel of divorce, but after months of counseling, reading, self-examination, and prayer, I finally came out the other end. I celebrated by throwing a marvelous dinner party which I prepared and served to nine of my best friends. (Think Babette's Feast to get the idea.) I saw the potential for a new beginning, energized by God's love and with renewed hope for the future. In divorce I became a broken failure, but also real. This is not the way I would have planned my life, but God used this opportunity to humble me and help me come to a deeper reality, and from there I was able to help others in their grief. God lifts us up and sends people to meet us in our brokenness; we remember the pain, but God is able to restore us to wholeness. Then we have the opportunity, with all of our imperfections, to become instruments of compassion and reconciliation for others who are also broken and hurting.

Brenan Manning writes, "Anyone God uses significantly is always deeply wounded . . . We are, each and every one of us, insignificant people whom God has called and graced to use in a significant way . . . On the last day, Jesus will look us over not for medals, diplomas or honors, but for scars."[1] Pope Francis says, "I prefer a Church which is bruised, hurting and dirty because it has been out on the streets."[2] Paul writes in his epistle to the Hebrews, "Endure hardship as discipline; God is treating you as sons. For what son is not disciplined by his father." (Hebrews 12:7).

For some reason, we humans have an unhealthy tendency to ruminate on the past. We can spend precious time regretting our mistakes and blaming ourselves and others. To get stuck in disappointments and losses of the past is to miss opportunities to engage in the present. The drag of the past is like pulling a cart with rusted axles or riding a bicycle with a brake pad rubbing on the wheel.

After misfortune or tragedy, God clearly doesn't want us to remain mired in self-pity and regret. God wants to use each of us as an imperfect instrument of blessing and hope in what sometimes seems to be a dark world. The light and love that we project is not our own, but God's reflected glory, shining forth despite our own brokenness and inadequacies.

As a physician and surgeon I have been acutely aware of the continuum between physical, mental, and spiritual health. I could predict that the patients with positive attitudes would usually heal the fastest after surgery. I was more concerned about those who did little to take care of their physical health (weight issues, poor diet, smoking, little exercise), especially if they came in to the clinic with a negative attitude. I remember one patient in particular who let everyone know what was wrong with the clinic and its personnel from the moment she stepped inside the front door. We could feel her icy blast of negativity all the way back into the exam rooms.

All of us encounter such individuals, and all of us experience stress, hardship, and tragedy in our lives. It is part of the human condition. Whatever our circumstances, we tend to worry and at times feel overwhelmed by the stress of our lives. We may feel like we can barely keep our head above water as the pressures of our job, family, finances, and other demands swirl around us. For some people the stress seems overwhelming, and it leads to clinical anxiety

1. Manning, *Ruthless Trust*, 48.
2. Francis, "Evangelii Gaudium," para. 49.

and/or depression. We may turn to alcohol or drugs in an attempt to blunt the pain, or we may turn inward, becoming self-absorbed just to get through the day. We feel defensive with the onslaught of competing interests that demand our time and attention. We may feel if we don't push ourselves harder, we just may not make it.

This scenario is a very human failing but quite the opposite of what God intends for us. We may have little control over some of the demands on our lives (our family, our work, etc.) and not know how to get ourselves out of the trap, but in other ways we may be able to unpack our schedules. My three children came to me one Saturday morning after I returned from a university board meeting and said through their tears, "Dad, you are just too busy." They were right, and I resigned from the board that day.

It is healthy and necessary to push the pause button when we feel overwhelmed. We all need to regroup at times and do some reflection about whether we are making the best use of our time and talents. Our lives are a gift from God, and we should not squander our time in a frenetic pursuit of prestige or money or position. Sin is anything that separates us from the love of God, and stress is one of those triggers that effectively block our connection to God.

Jesus invites us, "Come to me all you who are weary and burdened, and I will give you rest. Take my yoke upon you and learn from me, for I am gentle and humble in heart, and you will find rest for your souls. For my yoke is easy and my burden is light" (Matthew 11:28–30).

The expression about human life "from dust to dust" signifies that we start as atoms and end up as atoms; it is just our spirit that lives on. If you are like me, you have likely questioned whether this is all there is to life. Is it just random chance that these atoms formed into a human shape according to some genetic code? Or is there more to the story? I believe there is a much larger dimension of which we are only vaguely aware.

I have experienced so many serendipitous events in my life—some trivial, some significant—that I cannot believe that they were just chance encounters. When I was a teenager riding a motor scooter too fast on rain-slicked pavement with a date behind me, the scooter began to skid out from underneath us as I negotiated a curve. I could feel us going down, and then just as suddenly the scooter defied gravity and righted itself. Somehow, inexplicably, disaster was averted.

Another time I was running in the dark early one morning on an Israeli kibbutz on the Lebanese border. Suddenly a Doberman came bounding out of the darkness directly toward me. I felt totally vulnerable in my shorts and T-shirt and knew I had made a terrible mistake. As I stopped and stared in terror, a wondrous thing happened. The vicious dog abruptly stopped just ten yards away, and simply watched me. With cold beads of sweat on my brow, I very quietly sidled by.

A third incident came when I lived on a rural farm and enjoyed running on a country road. I knew the road well and knew there was a high, solid, wooden fence that jutted out right to the pavement, undoubtedly in violation of building codes. As I ran one day I couldn't shake the thought of a speeding car racing down the road past this fence. The feeling was so intense that when I reached the fence, I stopped and peered around the wooden structure. To my horror I watched as a car went speeding past just inches from the protruding fence. I was left emotionally shaken, but physically unscathed and immensely grateful.

One dark, black night I was driving into town from my farm, and came to the railroad tracks on Sawmill Road. There are no gates or warning lights at this rural crossing. I stopped like I always do, looked both ways, saw nothing and heard nothing. As I was about to step on the gas, I had a sixth sense that something was amiss. I peered into the night and suddenly realized that the towering side of a black railcar loomed above me, stalled on the tracks. This was back in the days when railcars were not required to have any warning lights or reflectors on their sides. I was just a few feet from running into a wall of steel, perhaps even being trapped under the boxcar amidst the wheels. With great relief I backed the car up, turned around, and drove to town by another route.

Another example of serendipity is forever etched in my mind. I was taking a load of yard clippings to the landfill using my neighbor's pickup. My son was about three and wanted to go along for the ride. The old pickup had no seat belts, back in an era when seat-belts were not required for older vehicles. We got to the dump and I backed the pickup to the edge of a ten-foot-deep trench that had been bulldozed for yard debris. I put the pickup in park, but discovered the parking break no longer worked. I lowered the tailgate and was shoveling debris into the trench, when suddenly the pickup started to roll backward toward the trench with my son inside. He had evidently shifted the transmission out of park into neutral. I tried to get into the cab, but didn't have time to open the door. Then, miraculously, the heavy pickup came to a stop at the brink of the pit, held up by nothing more than a twig. One moment I was sure I was about to lose my son, and the next he was alive and well, both of us in tears. After getting him to safety, I slowly inched the pickup forward out of harms way. I was one extremely grateful dad.

Are such incidents just happenstance? Perhaps, but I don't think so. Call it God's grace, or guardian angels, or whatever you like. My guess is that each of us has experienced phenomena that cannot be explained by scientific principles or the laws of nature. I believe there is a spiritual dimension to our existence, of which we are largely unaware, but which will be revealed upon our death. At that moment of transition, I expect we will experience an incredible "Aha" moment of clarity and understanding.

I suspect you may have had such experiences without recognizing the hand of God at work. I believe that God has been looking after each of us throughout our lives. In fact the psalmist says that God knows us before we are born (Psalm 139). We have likely shrugged off these events as happenstance, or luck, or good fortune. When we look back and put these pieces together, we may see a pattern of God at work, sowing seeds and seeking growth of our spiritual connection. When we "get it," realizing God's hand at work, it can be transformative, like Paul's revelation or conversion on the road to Damascus (Acts 9). God has been gently and patiently knocking at our door over most of our lives in seemingly insignificant and occasionally dramatic ways.

I was a student for what seemed an eternity of training—first college and then medical school, followed by five years of specialty training. When I would return home from school, I often left New

Haven or Charlottesville after classes and had to drive many hours to reach my family home in Princeton, New Jersey. Exhausted and hungry I would pull into the driveway late at night. The good news was that the porch light was always lit, and the front door always unlocked. I would quietly open the door, lock it gently behind me, and tiptoe across the front hall to the kitchen. And the best part was that my mother always left something delectable to eat, like a generous slice of lemon meringue pie, on the kitchen counter or in the refrigerator.

I think God is like that, waiting for us to come home with the lights on and a welcome embrace of love. Whether or not we are aware of it, God has been caring about us our whole lives. As imperfect as we are, through good times and bad, God has never stopped loving us.

Personally, I am willing and grateful to turn over my life with all of its worries and struggles to God. We have the choice to accept God's immense healing power and know that this is more than enough. When we align ourselves with the Almighty, most of our stressors seem far less important. The old is washed away and we take on a new life in the Spirit. In most churches this dynamic is symbolized by baptism.

Everywhere we are, God is there too. Our calling is to be in ongoing conversation with God through prayer, meditation, and an awareness of God's presence in all things. Even the darkest moments can be redeemed by God's love. Paul said, "Therefore we do not lose heart. Though outwardly we are wasting away, yet inwardly we are being renewed day by day. For our light and momentary troubles are achieving for us an eternal glory that far outweighs them all. So we fix our eyes not on what is seen, but on what is unseen. For what is seen is temporary, but what is unseen is eternal" (2 Corinthians 4:16–18).

CHAPTER 3

Seeking God

WE ARE CALLED TO seek the Lord with all our heart, soul, mind, and strength (Mark 12:30; Luke 10:27). How few of us actually follow this dictum, and yet it is basic to reaching our full human potential. To seek God as part of our human experience is how we are designed or wired. We have a hole in our being that can only be filled by God. We will never be whole, be satisfied, or be fulfilled until we have encountered God. Charles Gutenson writes, "Since God has created us for relationship, there is no other basis for our genuine fulfillment apart from relationship with God. All other alternative ways of pursuing fulfillment are illusory."[1]

It may be hard for us to believe that God would actually want to have a relationship with us. Doesn't God have better things to do? Are we worthy of God's personal attention? The reality is that it's not about us being worthy, but of God choosing to be in relationship with us, traveling with us though the joys and challenges of life. This is God's grace, a term that infers that God's love is neither deserved nor limited. God chooses to share God's abundance through imperfect beings like you and me. Can it be that God can use ordinary people like us to implement God's divine purpose? How remarkable that we are to be instruments of God's justice and mercy!

In chapter 2 we discussed that all of us are wounded and struggling as we make our way through life. At times we feel

1. Gutenson, *Christians and the Common Good*, 49.

overwhelmed, insecure, and defensive. As we cope with difficulties, we may try to make ourselves feel superior by pointing out the differences between ourselves and others: male/female, citizen/foreigner, black/white, attractive/plain, disabled/healthy, conservative/liberal. Categorizing others according to superficial traits and tribal identities is a way for our little minds to simplify the complexity of our world. It also allows us to designate some people as inferior or as outsiders. The more we accentuate differences, the more we are sure that we are right, just, and superior. Finding fault with others encourages us to treat them with distain or prejudice. The reality is that we are all children of God, intensely loved by our Creator. We have far more in common than we have differences with each other. We can break down barriers by treating others as family: brothers and sisters, parents and children. Our interconnection with others reminds me of the neighborhood road sign that reads, "Drive like your children live here."

When I admit to my own brokenness and imperfections, I am able to humbly ask God to take charge of my life. It goes something like this: "I've made a mess of things and need your forgiveness and help." Note there is little theology here, no religious ritual, no priest or minister, just a direct connection with the indwelling God. To ask forgiveness is so simple and yet so profound. As Cistercian monk Thomas Keating wrote, "We must first recognize our desperate need for God's healing before we can experience his infinite mercy. The deeper the experience of God's mercy, the more compassion we will have for others."[2]

By saying yes to God's presence in our lives, we feel immense gratitude and tend to live more in the present moment, not worrying about the past or the future. Franciscan Monk Richard Rohr states, "True spirituality is not a search for perfection, or control, or the door to the next world; it is a search for divine union *now*."[3] When we allow God to be central in our lives, we walk lightly with an easy step, full of gratitude. We come alive and delight in people and situations, as well as feeling their hurt and struggles. The path

2. Keating, *Daily Reader*, 125.
3. Rohr, *Naked Now*, 16.

may still be rocky, but there is little that can overwhelm us because we are not walking alone. When we live for God, we feel connected to an infinite source of love, blessed with God's abundance, at peace with ourselves, and full of compassion for others. As we open ourselves to God's love, we find it becomes infectious, filling us and spilling over to infect others. We discover we are able to connect to other people's hopes, fears, joys, and disappointments. We don't mind sharing our vulnerabilities, because God's love makes our own little egos relatively insignificant. When we connect with the Almighty, we are not to store up God's love but to give it away recklessly. Jesus squandered himself in radical self-giving, pouring himself out for the needs of others. Our greatest joy and privilege is to reach out and share God's love.

We started a free medical clinic on Saturdays at Trinity Covenant Church in Salem, Oregon, affiliated with the already successful Salem Free Medical Clinic downtown. Our congregation approved the clinic over objections of some naysayers who claimed the church classrooms would be contaminated with infections and the carpets would be stained with blood! In fact, we were able to show that after our cleanup crew had wiped down the rooms, the facility was cleaner than at the start of the day. We saw a great variety of patients, most of whom were unemployed and some of whom were undocumented. To us they were all just patients deserving of medical care and counseling. The volunteer staff and patients prayed together in a large circle at the start of each clinic, and personal prayer was offered to, but never imposed on, each of the patients.

I particularly remember one delightful patient, Mark, who was so moved by the healing ministry of the clinic that he returned to serve as a volunteer, later joined the church, and came to be chair of the church's building and grounds committee. The ripple effect of the free clinic spread far and wide across our community and inspired another church to do likewise.

God wants us to flourish, to live life with abundance, to be fully invested in God's creation, and to share in the redemption of the world. God wants us to partner in bringing God's kingdom to Earth. Thomas Keating put it beautifully: "We are called to be stewards of divine love."[4] God is the master planner; we are the workers in the vineyard. Whatever our talents and circumstances, we are called to be an integral part of God's plan. We never know how God may use us, and what may be the effect of our words and actions.

All of us have been on a cell phone call and suddenly lost the connection. "Can you hear me now?" used to be the question of the Verizon guy in commercial ads. Likewise, most of us get disconnected from God all too often. It's usually more gradual, almost imperceptible, like we inadvertently turned off the ringer and sent God to voicemail. At other times we aren't connected to God at all, like the phone is on airplane mode or turned off altogether.

When I am disconnected or unplugged from God, my day doesn't go well. I feel aimless, adrift, and self-absorbed. My interactions with others remain superficial and not fully engaged. By contrast, when I connect with God through prayer and meditation, I feel more fully alive and present. The more I feel God's presence—light, hope, compassion, love—the more it spills over to those I encounter along the way. I sometimes volunteer as an overnight host in a homeless shelter at a downtown church. Two volunteers share the responsibility to be sure that guests get what they need and that no one is disruptive during the night. When I feel God's presence in my life, I am genuinely interested in the guests and want to get to know them and hear their stories. I share with them, ask many questions, and we laugh and play together.

But occasions arise when I have been pushing hard, am burned out and feel disconnected from God. Feeling alone and empty, I know I need to recharge my batteries and fill up the tank. God is my filling station, and there's only one grade of fuel—"supreme." Through prayer and meditation God is able to renew my spirit. To illustrate one such low point, let me share the following entry in my spiritual journal from November 15, 2009:

> I'm at the Mt. Angel Shalom Center, depleted, exhausted, burned out. I'm carrying a lot of inner pain. Everyone seems so distant, including my friends and my wife. I call

4. Keating, *Daily Reader*, 333.

out to God and the words are lost in a dark void. I feel so
alone. I beg God to hear my cry. I hear the recording of a
beautiful anthem in the room next to mine. The singing
soothes my troubled soul. God is finding a way to get
through to me. My tears flow, and I begin to feel some
peace. I feel buoyed up, supported like a float on the
water. Why do I have to keep undergoing these times of
torment and darkness? Is it to identify with others who
are in pain or going through difficult times? Do I need
to struggle because that is part of the human condition,
including Jesus' life on earth? Does my faith grow stron-
ger when I bottom out and reach out to God with all my
heart and soul? I have no idea. Just hold me tight, God;
you are my refuge and my strength.

In the latter half-century of her life, Mother Teresa felt distant from God. In letters to her superiors she wrote, "As for me,
the silence and the emptiness is so great, that I look and do not see,
listen and do not hear . . ."[5] But during these several decades until
her death, Mother Teresa continued her commitment to serve the
poorest of the poor in Kolkata, India. She remained faithful to her
calling despite feeling so alone. She knew that God is faithful, even
if sometimes the calls get dropped.

5. Kolodiejchuk, *Mother Teresa*, 288.

CHAPTER 4

On God's Team

DOES GOD CHOOSE US or do we choose to center our lives on God? Some years ago I made a fundamental commitment to turn my life over to God—my work, my time, my relationships, my very being. Living in faith can seem like the ultimate "going out on a limb," where we give up control of our lives and become vulnerable. I had the sense that this change of heart was not my doing, but initiated by God; I was just the grateful recipient. I began to see the world through God's eyes with love and compassion, and I became less judgmental about my own faults (no dearth of faults here) and those of others.

It seems that God is the driving force behind this connection, and God wants to be in relationship with each of us. We can choose to recognize God's love, freely given and without qualification, or we can choose to ignore it. But we are still part of God's design and have the opportunity to open ourselves to God's presence at any time. Jesus said, "My commandment is this: Love each other as I have loved you . . . You did not choose me, but I chose you and appointed you to go and bear fruit—fruit that will last" (John 15:12, 16).

During my student years away from home, I would often call home on Sunday afternoons. I would call collect, which, for younger readers, means I would call the operator, who would ask my parents if they would accept the long-distance charges. I marveled that whenever I called, no matter what activity I might be interrupting, my parents were glad to hear from me and happy to accept the charges. I think God is like that—always wanting to hear from us at any time of the day or night, a welcoming and caring presence at the other end of our prayer.

God wants to reach out to each of us like a parent wants to connect with his/her child. God's love is not limited by our past mistakes, or by our race, culture, schooling, or gifts. We are not deserving of God's grace by our righteousness, nor are we rejected for our misdeeds. All are invited to share at God's table; no one is excluded.

The reality is that there is a divine ember burning within each of us. We can choose to fan this flame, or we can choose to just let it smolder. Two followers of Jesus did not recognize him on the road to Emmaus, but they noted, "Were not our hearts burning within us?" (Luke 24:32). When we feel God's call, we have the opportunity to open our hearts, explore the mystery, talk with friends about their faith, read books about spirituality, listen to sermons and tapes, and most of all, pray. A number of helpful books are listed in the bibliography. Your calling is a great gift, a treasure to be cultivated and nurtured. Faith starts as a small seed, no bigger than a mustard seed, which one day may flourish into a grand tree.

Once when I was a high school student riding the Pennsylvania Railroad train to New York, the gentleman next to me turned and asked, "Brother, have you been saved?" I was a bit flustered, and my response was something like, "Well, I think so." At that I buried my nose in Tolstoy's *War and Peace*, effectively cutting off further conversation.

What does it mean to be saved or to be born again? These pithy but loaded expressions mean different things to different people: an evangelical, a mainline Christian, or a member of another faith tradition. To atheists or agnostics these are hot-button expressions that turn them off and often shut down further discussion. Religious people can be full of jargon and glib clichés that mean little outside their own circle and often are counterproductive.

"Have you been saved?" is really asking the wrong question. The question needs to be, "Have you joined God's team?" Do you care about the poor, sick, lonely, hungry, homeless, strangers, immigrants, prisoners, minorities, and the physically and mentally handicapped? These were clearly Jesus' concerns, and if we are followers of Jesus, they need to be our concern as well. We need to do our part to address the needs of the here and now. Jesus instructed his disciples to pray to God, "Your kingdom come on earth as it is in heaven."

I believe that a pivotal moment often occurs when we first encounter God in a meaningful way, sometimes called conversion. It is when we let go of our own egos and ask God to take charge of our lives. It is recognition that God has always been part of us, despite our resistance and denial. Richard Rohr writes, "You too are both human and divine, as Jesus came to reveal and model for us. To hold these two seeming contraries together is to be 'saved.'"[1] To be saved or converted is to surrender to God's spirit and to draw upon the divine power of love and compassion. For Christians Jesus is the link revealing God in human form, and when we accept Jesus as our savior, we are acknowledging God's living presence.

Transformation is not for the timid or faint of heart. It takes a certain determination and persistence to keep on questioning, listening, and searching. Conversion is not merely a one-time event, although we may be able to date the time when our spiritual journey first began. It is not a done deal, an end in itself, but rather is the beginning of our transformation to the will of God. It is the first step in discipleship, an ongoing process of yielding to God, with missteps and asking forgiveness along the way, and requiring us to recommit ourselves daily.

The reality is that nothing is more profound and gratifying than to respond to God's call on our lives. It beats all our petty, shallow goals of success, affluence, and fame. We are primed to be born of the Spirit; it is part of our human DNA, a fertile garden waiting to grow. But like with any new experience, we can expect some highs and lows with lots of stumbling on our spiritual journey.

Christianity is not simply a self-help religion or a twelve-step program. It is not about me, namely God coming to solve my problems, but about my joining God's team to understand my role in

1. Rohr, *Just This*, 88.

fostering God's kingdom on Earth. As a Christian, we become a new person, reflecting God's love with humility and gratitude. Paul writes, "I no longer live, but Christ lives in me. The life I live in the body, I live by faith in the son of God, who loved me and gave himself for me" (Galatians 2:20).

Conversion to Christianity is not to be taken lightly. Shane Claiborne and John M. Perkins write, "We've gotten a lot of people who have supposedly asked Jesus into their hearts, but they are not living with any gratitude. They've got Jesus working for them instead of doing his work in the world . . . Jesus has no hands but my hands and your hands . . . We are all that God has to reach out to the homeless and the poor in our society."[2]

To be followers of Jesus is to prioritize prayer like Jesus. Ongoing prayer and meditation is necessary to seek God's will for our lives. The Gospels are full of accounts of Jesus going off alone to pray in a quiet place, and we are to do likewise. In fact, Jesus spent so much time in prayer that I sometimes wonder when he had time to sleep!

What God has in mind for us is to become receiving stations and conduits of God's grace. As Richard Rohr says, "We slowly learn the right frequencies that pick up the signal . . . There is someone dancing with you, and you are not afraid of making mistakes."[3] The result is that we no longer feel solely responsible for our lives. We don't have to keep pushing ourselves and striving alone, because we know we are yoked to a higher power. We see ourselves in a different light, as humble, awed, and grateful servants of the Lord.

It takes time and intention, but the rewards of tuning into God's frequency are like nothing else on Earth. Our caring and compassion for others is a manifestation of God's love in action. Our connection to the Divine is what gives us strength and fortitude and will bear fruit far beyond anything our egos could ever accomplish. A natural consequence is that we often want to share the peace and joy with which we are blessed. "Freely you have received, freely give" (Matthew 10:8).

2. Claiborne, *Follow Me to Freedom*, 123.

3. Rohr, *Naked Now*, 23.

We should relish our faith journey: it may well prove to be the most exciting adventure of our lives. Our response to God's call will forever change us and is likely to change those with whom we interact. This is not an exclusive club—all are invited, and all can be used for God's purpose. But know that if we choose to live out our faith, we can expect to engender derision and criticism from some of our friends and acquaintances. It comes with the territory in a society that prides itself on rational thought, intellect, prestige, and affluence. Skeptics abound when our priorities do not reflect the conventional wisdom of the day. But there's a silver lining: if we are challenged by others along the way, they are helping us to grow and mature in our faith. When we rub up against resistance, it helps us to hone our beliefs, and it motivate us to probe deeper into the spiritual dimension.

John Stumbo, formerly the head pastor of a prominent Salem, OR, church, was a marathon runner and in excellent physical shape. With no warning, over the course of several days he found himself paralyzed, unable even to swallow. He had to go on life support as multiple organs failed, and it was believed he was close to death. Despite the best medical providers and diagnostic equipment at Oregon's leading medical center, his doctors were unable to come up with a diagnosis. The condition was unrelenting, persisting through many months of hospitalization.

During convalescence at home when he was eventually able to speak, John showed no hint of self-pity or resentment for his illness and forced retirement. Quite the contrary, he said, "Some people talk about their glass being half full or half empty. Actually my cup just keeps overflowing." He continued, "You don't get to choose all the circumstances that happen in your life, but you do get to choose how you respond." All of us will experience tough times; it is part of the human condition. The question is how will we respond to adversity and will it shake our faith?

Later John wrote a book in which he confided, "I'm not on the journey I ever expected to be on, I don't have all my questions about it answered, and I don't know where it leads; but if I can be passionate for life all the way to the end and praise my God along the way,

I'm convinced that the journey will be good."[4] John has made a full recovery and currently serves as president of the U.S. Christian and Missionary Alliance.

Five years before his illness, Pastor Stumbo composed this poem:

IF YOU FIND ME

If you find me on the side of a mountain trail or a lonely road,
The soulless remains of a brain aneurysm or heart malfunction,
Grieve my absence, but please don't grieve my death or my life.

If you find my blood spilled upon some foreign soil, Bible in backpack,
message in heart,
Grieve my assailant but please don't question my going.

I will not be embalmed with those lifeless souls who died well before
their final death.
I will not be entombed with the fear slaves who could not live because
they could not risk.

I will not be reckless, I will be guarded by wisdom,
But I refuse to guard my life so carefully that I cannot push off
from shore.

I choose to embrace all of life that righteousness will allow,
To set sail at the slightest breath of wind,
To climb and taste, run and enjoy,
To pray and play with equal zeal.

So let any words that should be said, be said;
Make any memories that should be made,
Share any love that should be shared.

For I refuse to save my life or fear my death.
I will die living rather than live dying.

---

4. Stumbo, *Honest Look at a Mysterious Journey*, 276.

So if you find me suddenly gone,
Take comfort in knowing that this is the way I wanted to live,
Embracing life on earth one moment,
Embracing Life Himself, the next.[5]

5. Previously unpublished. Used with permission of the author.

CHAPTER 5

Pitfalls: Ego and Certitude

LIFE IS A DANCE between our ego and our spiritual self. These entities are sometimes labeled our false self and our true self. The false self is our petty, fragile, insecure ego, which takes offense when it feels threatened and can't stand to be slighted. It likes to feel important and respected and is easily upset, lashing out with righteous indignation when it feels we have been wronged. It doesn't like to admit our faults and inadequacies, our self-centeredness and imperfections, or to apologize to others. The ego wants to be in control, and is our biggest impediment to being open, vulnerable and available to the presence of God.

Our egos are a part of our development, what Richard Rohr calls "your launching pad: your body image, your job, your education, your clothes, your money, your car, your sexual identity, your success, and so on . . . They are a nice enough platform to stand on, but they are largely a projection of our self-image and our attachment to it."[1] Rohr points out that the false self or ego is not bad. It is necessary as far as it goes; it's just incomplete and doesn't go far enough. "When you are able to move beyond your False Self—at the right time and in the right way—*it will feel precisely like you have lost nothing*. In fact, it will feel like freedom and liberation. When

---

1. Rohr, *Immortal Diamond*, 28.

you are connected to the Whole, you no longer need to protect or defend the mere part."[2]

Faith is about giving up our ego. It turns out that the ego that we so fiercely defend is not worth a hill of beans. Letting go of it is a relief and gives us license *not* to defend our positions or justify ourselves. Since the ego doesn't need to be stroked anymore, we can be present in the moment and just let other people's opinions of us wash over us without feeling threatened. Contrast this to narcissists, who have an insatiable ego and grandiose sense of self-importance, while lacking empathy for the feelings and needs of others. These unfortunate folks have a strong sense of entitlement, are preoccupied with their own success, and need constant admiration and flattery.

By letting go of ego, we are able to focus our attention and energy on drawing closer to God. What we are giving up is insignificant compared to being in relationship with the Creator, the ultimate source of all that is. We no longer live for ourselves, but we live for God like hired hands in God's vineyard. We seek to implement God's plan, which may not be clear at first, but which may become discernible over time through prayer and meditation.

Our faith journey entails repeatedly emptying ourselves of pride, while our ego tries to sneak back through a side door. Over time our ego becomes less insistent, and we experience God's closeness more readily and more frequently. Communion with God becomes a natural part of who we are. Rohr writes, "Eventually we can live our life from calm inner awareness and acceptance."[3]

In early adulthood, we are so busy getting educated, launching our careers, and starting a family that we rush through our days and often take friends and family for granted. With age comes wisdom and the realization that the important things in life are deep and abiding connections with other people. Nineteenth-century evangelist Henry Drummond wrote, "You will find as you look back upon your life that the moments that stand out, the moments when you have really lived, are the moments when you have done things

2. Rohr, *Immortal Diamond*, 28.
3. Rohr, *Just This*, 58.

in a spirit of love."[4] Jack Kornfield puts it this way: "The things that matter most in our lives are not fantastic or grand. They are moments when we touch one another, when we are there in the most attentive or caring way. This simple and profound intimacy is the love we all long for."[5]

Many people, especially we males, tend to live in our heads: what we think is who we are. We develop ideas and tenaciously defend our positions as if they were the core of our being. But this is not the way of Jesus, who lived not in his head, but in his heart. He reached out with empathy and compassion to everyone in need, and was outspoken, passionate, and sometimes moved to anger. He was literally and figuratively touched by all who sought him out, including a woman who dared to touch his robe to cure her hemorrhaging (Luke 8:33–34).

The motivation for the first half of my life was achievement: accomplishing goals and milestones around education, work, family, and various organizations. As a type-A personality, I'm sure I was a tough nut for God to crack! While my goals were worthy, they also sidetracked me from slowing down, listening, and developing a closer relationship with the Almighty. In general, the first half of life is about developing an identity, including ethnicity, schooling, occupation, friends, and often marriage and parenthood, to name a few characteristics that define who we are. When our major focus is on success, achievement, and gaining respect, our feelings of self-importance may undermine any hope of a closer relationship with God.

Ideally the second half of life is about letting go of our persona and surrendering our identity to a higher power, i.e., aligning ourselves with God's values and God's plan. Jesus said, "Whoever finds his life will lose it, and whoever loses his life for my sake will find it" (Matthew 10:39). Think about how we spend much of our lives acquiring bigger homes and material possessions, and then we spend our latter years downsizing and getting rid of our accumulated "stuff." Thank goodness for garage sales, Craigslist, and eBay!

4. Drummond, "Greatest Thing in the World," a speech.
5. Kornfield, *Path with Heart*, 14.

When our parents die, we are dismayed if they haven't downsized and cleaned their home of all its clutter. The time for a course correction on materialism vs. spirituality is whenever we are ready to make God our top priority.

Jesus said, "Blessed are the poor in spirit, for theirs is the kingdom of heaven" (Matthew 5:3). How incredible! We have to humble and empty ourselves (be poor in spirit) to be available to receive God's grace. We need to admit that we are flawed, wounded, and broken. When I see my ego as the stumbling block that it is, I am able to renounce it, ask forgiveness, and move on. I don't take myself so seriously since there is nothing to protect and defend. I feel liberated from my bogus ego and can open myself to God's healing presence. I begin to see God everywhere, in the smile of a child, in the music of a songbird, in the eyes of an elderly person, in the exquisite colors of a sunset. I feel free to walk in the light without a lot of baggage.

Our reality is so different from God's reality. Our true self is centered in God and gives control over to God. There is no need to be controlling; someone else is in control. The true self will not get defensive; it has nothing to defend. It's about trust, letting go, and turning our lives over to a higher power. Transformed people don't need power, prestige, or possessions. They are not grasping for more, but are grounded in the sense that they have plenty. They are not perfect—far from it—but they are centered in God, allowing them to be free and whole. They need less and less to make them happy because they already have what they need.

In the process of our transformation, God may have to destabilize our ego, often through suffering and humiliation. God has to let us fail, as happened with my marriage. It sometimes takes just such a cataclysmic event before we are willing to let go, surrender our ego, and trust in God. Finding our true self requires an inward journey that lets go of many preconceived notions. It is amidst our pain, fears, sorrows, and aloneness that we may feel the love of God, and tap into God's healing presence. Elizabeth O'Connor has put it,

"When we are able to keep company with our own fears and sorrows, we are shown the way to go."[6]

The divine presence was here all along, but we were too blind to feel God's spirit at the core of our being. The true self trusts in God, who transforms us, liberates us, and takes control of our lives. God's way is abundant, and it allows us to live in fullness and wholeness. This is the peace that the world cannot give, the joy that the world cannot take away.

As our own defense mechanisms crumble, and as we become more accepting of God's grace, we also become far more tolerant of others. We accept them as they are and not as we think they should be. We no longer project our agenda, attachments, aversions, and demands on them. They are every bit as flawed as we are, and we can empathize with them and love them without judgment, as God has loved us.

While our ego is a major stumbling block to spirituality, another is a false sense of certitude about our religious views. We are so much more than our thoughts and opinions, which the false self fiercely defends as truth. None of us knows more than a tiny fraction of God's truth, and we need a healthy dose of humble pie when we share our religious views with others. We simply don't know *the way*, and in fact there are likely to be multiple paths to the Almighty. As strongly as we may feel about our beliefs, we need to be open to other avenues to access God's love and forgiveness.

Certitude about religion has been a recipe for self-interest, power, and sometimes violence. It has fueled many a war. When we feel sure that we are on God's side, we avoid our shadow side, and defend our religion with dualistic thinking (right/wrong, good/evil, like/dislike, saved/unsaved). When we feel certain and self-righteous, arrogance so frequently follows. From the life and teachings of Jesus, we see that a smug, self-satisfied attitude is fraught with spiritual pitfalls. Jesus railed against the scribes and Pharisees who pigeonholed religion into rules, rituals, and formulas.

I come from a Christian perspective but don't feel that Christianity holds an exclusive right of access to God. I continually learn

6. O'Connor, *Cry Pain, Cry Hope*, 84.

from my Jewish, Muslim, and Buddhist brothers and sisters who are seeking answers to the unfathomable mystery of life through different channels. The words they use to describe their faith sound remarkably familiar, and I believe God values their connection as much as those of us who call ourselves Christians. We do them a disservice if we claim that there is only one true religion and one pathway to God. Doesn't God want to embrace all God's children, whether or not they are followers of Jesus?

One biblical passage in the Gospel of John gives an exclusive perspective that has been used to justify the concept that Jesus is the only path to God: "I tell you the truth, I am the gate for the sheep. All who ever came before me were thieves and robbers, but the sheep did not listen to them. I am the gate; whoever enters through me will be saved" (John 10:7–9). While saying that his followers may be saved, Jesus doesn't say that people of other faiths will be excluded. In fact Jesus goes on to say, "I have other sheep that are not of this sheep pen" (John 10:16). Who would doubt that the Old Testament patriarchs and prophets are exalted in the kingdom of God, despite not being "Christians"? Jesus said, "I say to you that many will come from the east and the west, and will take their places at the feast with Abraham, Isaac and Jacob in the kingdom of heaven" (Matthew 8:11). Did not Moses and Elijah appear with Jesus at the transfiguration (Matthew 17, Mark 9)? Martin Luther King Jr. remarked in a speech that he considered Gandhi (a Hindu) to be "the greatest Christian of the modern world."

I think well-meaning, righteous Christians are on shaky ground if they believe that only Christians will enter the heavenly kingdom. None of us know where we are going in the afterlife, and I suspect we may be amazed at the array of "non-Christians" who are likely to be seated before the throne of God. Jesus' inclusive message typically emphasized outsiders as the heroes of his parables. To illustrate who is our neighbor, Jesus picked a Samaritan, at a time when Jews considered Samaritans as ethnically and religiously inferior (Luke 10:29–37). Another time Jesus told of a despised tax collector who was justified before God, whereas a Pharisee was not (Luke 18:9–14). Jesus spoke with a Samaritan woman at Jacob's well about her lifestyle and faith, clearly breaking with Jewish social mores (John 4:4–42).

When Jesus taught at his home synagogue in Nazareth, he recalled that the prophets Elijah and Elisha ministered to the needs of non-Jews, rather than Israelites, when all were suffering from hunger and leprosy (Luke 4:16–30). The implication that God favors outsiders, not God's "chosen people," enraged the home congregation to the point that they attempted to kill Jesus by throwing him off a cliff. Jesus healed the mental illness of a Gerasene wild man, considered by Jews to be a heathen (Mark 5:1–20; Luke 8:26–39). Jesus defended and praised a "sinful" woman who washed his feet with her tears and anointed them with perfume (Luke 7:36–50). Jesus healed the daughter of a Roman centurion, the occupying enemy of Israel (Matthew 8:5–13). Numerous other examples indicate that Jesus welcomed all into the kingdom of God.

Speaker and author Brian McLaren writes, "I've been convinced that Christian identity involves both *witness*—graciously and confidently sharing our unique, Christ-centered message, and *with-ness*—experiencing solidarity with people of other faiths, worshipping in one another's presence and working together for the common good."[7]

It is said that "Mother Teresa never tried to convert a Muslim or Hindu to Christianity. She told the sisters that their job was not to talk about Jesus, or even promote Jesus, but to *be* Jesus."[8] What a concept! We are all in this together, whatever our faith tradition. Religion is a construct of humans, not of God. The clash of religions has caused incalculable misery and suffering over the centuries. We need to overcome religious and sectarian differences, and build on our common humanity and our collective search for meaning and purpose, through the grace of God.

7. McLaren, *Why Did Jesus, Moses, the Buddha, and Mohammed Cross the Road?*, 242.

8. Rohr, *Naked Now*, 100.

CHAPTER 6

Encountering God in Daily Living

AT A SMALL BUSH hospital in Sierra Leone, West Africa, where I have volunteered on three occasions, I came face to face with what is important in life. In this poor country close to the equator, survival is fragile with life and death in precarious balance. The heat is oppressive, infectious diseases are rampant, and malnutrition of children is endemic. I witnessed many children die at the hospital, brought in by their parents as a last resort, too late for medical treatment.

I was walking across the waiting room when a desperate father thrust his young son into my arms. The child was feverish and unresponsive, and he was accompanied by an entourage of family members who were wailing, like people do at a wake. The family had come to our mission hospital in desperation after native healers and roadside "pharmacies" had failed to heal the boy. Against all odds we started an IV and began to give him antimalarial medication, but within the hour the boy had died. So tragic and so unnecessary.

Living in Sierra Leone took me way outside my comfort zone. Everything is different: extreme heat, unusual customs, multiple tribal languages, strange food, rampant illiteracy, subjugation of women, intermittent electricity, reckless driving, jungle sounds at night, and so much more. Cut off from familiar patterns of my daily routine, I felt vulnerable and alone. As a physician, I was frustrated by not being able to get an accurate medical history from patients who didn't even know their age, much less their current medications or their history of illness and surgery. I remember thinking: How can I help these people if they don't take any responsibility for their health? Oh, what a privileged and condescending point of view!

When all of our props and comforts are taken away, we are brought face to face with the reality of who we are in relationship to God. In many ways it is not a pretty sight. Much of our lives in this society seem so petty and shallow. They are about comforts and conveniences, financial security, success, our appearance, trivial interests in sports and entertainment, shopping, nutritious food, exercise, our hobbies and electronic gadgets, and our 401K retirement plan.

Much of my time in Portland is spent on committees and boards, setting policy but working a couple of steps removed from the neediest people in our community. If I am honest, I have to ask myself whether part of my motivation is seeking the respect of others and promoting my own public persona. In the African bush, there is no time or place for polishing one's self-image; no pretenses, just the basics of hard work and a will to survive. I went to Sierra Leone and came face to face with Jesus. The good news is that we don't have to go to Africa to do this. We can encounter Jesus among the poor under bridges, in migrant camps, at soup kitchens, and standing on street corners holding up cardboard signs.

Author, speaker, and activist Shane Claiborne says, "We need to see where God is at work and join in."[1] God's purpose needs to be our purpose. Jesus has no hands but my hands and your hands; we are all that God has to reach out to the homeless and the poor. Claiborne predicts, "We can be assured that an encounter with Jesus will mess us up and transform not only what we believe but who we are . . . even our very lives."[2]

We may encounter God in the most unexpected places and at times we least anticipate. God is everywhere in the ordinary and in the extraordinary if we but open our eyes and are receptive to

1. Claiborne, *Follow Me to Freedom*, 82.
2. Claiborne, *Follow Me to Freedom*, 93.

God's presence. God seems to be saying, "My world is a feast; enjoy, delight, laugh and appreciate all that I have set before you. Observe and sense my presence in all things, and it will transform your life. I am in the flowers of the field and in the sunsets, but also in the darkness of the ghettos. You will find me among the poor and sick, the forgotten and marginalized. Look for me and you will feel my presence."

Imagine living your life as if you are in God's presence at all times, which of course you are. When I sense God's presence, I live my life differently, expecting to find God's spirit in nearly all situations. My radar is turned on, and I begin to experience God in nature, in people, and in everyday encounters. I believe we are all spiritual beings who, by the grace of God, have been given the gift of physical life on Earth.

We need to let God's love wash over us, cleanse us, and make us whole; this is what we were made for. Our acceptance of this transformative process is what will change the world. "I only want to do the will of God" was the prayer of Jesus, his mother, Mary, and the apostle Paul, but it is not reserved for saints and mystics. Ideally everything we do and say should pass through this filter, and each of us can be a participant in helping to transform the world.

No human mind can grasp who or what God is. Mystics have described a "cloud of unknowing" that will always exist between us and God. I believe God is pure love, infinite and timeless from the first moment of creation. The divine spirit lives within each of us whether we choose to recognize it or not. The disconnection between God and us is not God's doing but the result of our own indifference and distraction. We need to nurture our spiritual connection, much like starting a fire with small wood shavings and gradually adding kindling until it burns brightly.

What I learned in Sierra Leone has changed my life. Ultimately each of us is called to be a source of light and love in the world. We are to love God with all of our heart, soul, mind, and strength and to love others with the compassion of Jesus. We are invited to tap into God's infinite source of love and truth. We may access only a small fraction of what God offers us, but even that will be sufficient to make all the difference. When we place ourselves in the hands of God, we experience gratitude and peace.

When I live life for myself, I am often defensive, driven, and judgmental, being critical of both myself and others. When I live for God, I live in God's abundance, knowing that I am blessed and loved. I feel full of gratitude and am drawn into relationships with others, wanting to share their joys and sorrows. Self-centeredness and self-promotion are replaced with a freedom in the Spirit and a sense of oneness with others.

I have a house on Orcas Island in the San Juan Islands of the Pacific Northwest. From my house I can see the Olympic Mountains to the southwest and the Canadian Gulf Islands to the northwest. This home is my spiritual retreat, located on a knoll where I feel close to God and removed from the many demands and distractions of life in the city. I recognize that this land once belonged to the Lummi Tribe (now the Lummi Nation) and am ashamed of the way that our forebears appropriated the land and relegated the tribes to swaths of less desirable land called reservations. Aptly named, as I bet the Indians had "reservations" about being forcibly settled on these lands. But the past is past, and while I recognize the injustices then and now, I try to make the most of the present. I have no control over the past; I hope I can have a small impact on the present and future.

On Orcas Island I struggle and wrestle with God, sometimes confronting God like the blowing wind in the Douglas fir trees overhead. But mostly I sit quietly and attentively on my window seat, like a bald eagle in a snag, as waves of gratitude wash over me. I have only the merest glimpse of union with the Divine, and yet even that changes my life fundamentally and unalterably. I am a new creation when bathed in the infinite love of the Creator.

If God is pure love, it doesn't make much sense to think that Jesus died to appease a vengeful God. The "atonement theory" says that Jesus was a blood sacrifice to atone for human's disobedience and sinfulness. As Franciscan monk Richard Rohr says, "Why would God need a 'blood sacrifice' before God could love what God had created? Is God that needy, unloving, rule-bound, and unforgiving? What would God ask of me if God demands violent blood sacrifice from God's only Son?"[3] "God did not need Jesus to die on the cross to decide to love humanity. God's love was infinite from the first moment of creation; the cross was Love's dramatic portrayal in space and time. Jesus was pure gift."[4]

Jesus died not to change God's mind about us but to change our minds about God. Jesus taught us to stop trying to earn God's good grace by following laws and rules, and making showy displays of piety. Jesus came to demonstrate not a vengeful God but a God who acts out of pure love, even to the point of dying in pain and rejection and humility on a cross. Jesus revealed God's infinite love for humankind, dying to the sins of the world, and overcoming death with resurrection and new life in the Spirit. It provides hope that no matter how bleak the outlook for our world, God will overcome hatred, violence, and the misuse of power.

On the cross Jesus forgave his enemies, saying, "Forgive them, Father, for they do not know what they are doing" (Luke 23:34). Jesus not only preached that we should love our enemies, he showed us what this means through his life and death. We could not have a clearer image of sacrificial love.

3. Rohr, "Substitutionary Atonement."
4. Rohr, "Nonviolent Atonement."

CHAPTER 7

Who Is Jesus?

I BELIEVE JESUS IS the son of God, sent to reveal God's nature in human form. Jesus is "the image of the invisible God" (Colossians 1:15), sent as a pure gift to manifest God's graciousness. Through the life and teachings of Jesus, we gain a glimpse of God's love for all of humanity and for all of God's creation. Jesus is the personification of love, compassion, and forgiveness. To follow Jesus draws us toward lives of inner depth, prayer, reconciliation, and healing, i.e. closer to the heart of God. In the Sermon on the Mount, Jesus says blessed are the gentle, the merciful, and the peacemakers (Matthew 5). His response to enmity and rejection is love and forgiveness. In multiple biblical passages, his message to us is to follow him and do likewise.

Jesus' life modeled a human-divine union, which is our true nature. Many of us have lost the spiritual connection, but the good news is that God wants nothing more than to restore a close relationship with each of us. God's spirit within us is like a homing device that wants to re-establish a connection to God. We can't think ourselves into this relationship; it takes place on a heartfelt, intuitive, gut level where many of us, especially males, may choose not to go. In my experience, it is in times of quiet, humility, and openness that I can move beyond my distracting thoughts and petty concerns and into this deeper space.

We live in a society that values wealth, power, and prestige. From Botox to Beemers, we are told it's about looking good and being successful. By contrast, Jesus eschewed power and privilege. He taught and modeled another path, one of service to others, seeking reconciliation and social justice. His example embodied humility and powerlessness, living among the poor and marginalized, and dying naked and bleeding on a cross. He chose not an earthly kingdom, but to advocate for God's kingdom on Earth. He instructed his followers to live simply, to "take nothing for the journey except a staff—no bread, no bag, no money in your belts" (Mark 6:8).

God sent Jesus, God's only son, into the world to show how much God loved us, even to the point of humiliation, pain, and torture on a cross. Jesus is God's gift to demonstrate what pure love looks like in human form. Jesus is the ultimate example of selfless love, which is reckless, risks all, and spares nothing. In his time in the wilderness, Jesus didn't try to prove himself in self-serving ways. At the inception of his ministry, Jesus stood up in the synagogue in Nazareth and read from the prophet Isaiah, "'The Spirit of the Lord is on me, because he has anointed me to preach good news to the poor. He has sent me to proclaim freedom for the prisoners and recovery of sight for the blind, to release the oppressed, to proclaim the year of the Lord's favor.' Then he rolled up the scroll, gave it back to the attendant and sat down. The eyes of everyone in the synagogue were fastened on him, and he began by saying, 'Today this scripture is fulfilled in your hearing'" (Luke 4:18–21). What a dramatic and provocative start to his ministry!

Jesus preached and practiced status inversion among rich and poor, powerful and weak, pious and humble. Jesus tells a parable of a Pharisee and a tax collector. One lives a life of prestige and honor; the other is despised. It is the tax collector for whom Jesus feels compassion and mercy when the tax collector confesses, "God, have mercy on me, a sinner" (Luke 18:13). Jesus says, "For everyone who exalts himself will be humbled, and he who humbles himself will be exalted" (Luke 18:14). Jesus always sides with the poor and marginalized, those who are sick, vulnerable, and outcasts from society. Other examples include his parables of the rich man and Lazarus (Luke 16:19–31) and the Good Samaritan (Luke 10:30–37).

Mary, the mother of Jesus, understood this inverse perspective when she said of God:

> He has scattered those who are proud in their inmost thoughts.
> He has brought down rulers from their thrones
> but has lifted up the humble.
>
> (From the Magnificat, Luke 1:51–52)

Jesus' values run counter to the cultural norm of being male in our society, often associated with being strong, tough, assertive, confident, competitive, strong-willed, and macho. Instead Jesus demonstrated humility, gentleness, compassion, and obedience to God as primary values. He taught us that we have to be willing to lose ourselves to find ourselves, to be willing give up everything to gain everything. The more we give away of God's love, the more it is replenished. When we use our modest means and talents (loaves and fishes), God can perform miracles with what little we have.

Jesus seems less concerned with what someone *believes* than what someone *does*. In his book *White Awake*, Daniel Hill, pastor of Chicago's River City Community Church, points out that evangelical Christians encourage people to "invite Jesus into their hearts." While this is theologically sound, Hill indicates that this message is incomplete. He references New Testament scholar Klyne Snodgrass, who notes five places where Paul uses the language of Christ "in us" or "in me." By contrast, Paul uses the phrase "in Christ" an astonishing 164 times. "If our view of Christianity is limited to Christ being 'in me' or 'in us,' we will never have the theological resources to join him in works of reconciliation and justice. But if our view is expanded to see faith as fundamentally about being 'in Christ,' our framework changes. Our very identity is seen through the lens of being joined to Christ, and we look to participate in the kingdom work Jesus is always doing."[1]

Jesus chose the road of humble service and sacrificial suffering. He taught by example and by parables, demonstrating how we should treat others, particularly those on the margins of society. His call was to "follow me," not to "worship me." In our society Jesus' way is daunting for many, and is generally the road less traveled.

---

1. Hill, *White Awake*, 92–93.

It is easier to turn our eyes heavenward and worship a king than to follow in the footsteps of a poor, humble, itinerant rabbi. It is worrisome to me when some Christians emphasize the kingship of Jesus. The sign on the cross read, "Jesus, the King of the Jews," at the instruction of the Roman governor of Judea, but Jesus never sought an earthly kingdom during his ministry. When he rode into Jerusalem, he did so not on a white stallion, but on a lowly donkey colt. When Christians emphasize the temporal kingship of Jesus and speak in the language of conquest, it feeds into the perverse ideology of empire and dominance. The crusades of the eleventh and twelfth centuries become the Pax Americana of the twentieth and twenty-first centuries. Nowhere in Jesus' life and teachings do we find him advocating for temporal power and domination.

The kingdom of God is quite a different matter, and Jesus compares God's kingdom to a pearl of great value. "The kingdom of heaven is like a merchant looking for fine pearls. When he found one of great value, he went away and sold everything he had and bought it" (Matthew 13:45–46). We are to be willing to let go of everything to be in relationship with God. Nothing—neither riches, nor prestige, nor power, nor fame—is as important as the priceless treasure of our faith in God. As a homeless teacher with a small band of unassuming followers, there's no question where Jesus set his priorities.

In our materialistic society where wealth has become a prime motivator and holy grail for many people, it may seem disconcerting that Jesus was on the side of the poor. Some Christians have twisted Jesus' teachings into a rewards system where God blesses the faithful with material possessions. This "prosperity gospel" distortion of Jesus' teachings may appeal to a materialistic society: love the Lord and material riches will follow. But how crass to attempt to use God as a steppingstone to personal wealth!

If you look to Jesus to support your desire for material blessings, you will be sadly disappointed: "Woe to you who are rich, for you have already received your comfort" (Luke 6:24). Read the parable of the rich man and Lazarus, who sat at the rich man's gate longing to eat what fell from the rich man's table (Luke 16:19–31). To say the least, things don't go well for the rich man.

Jesus taught, "Watch out! Be on your guard against all kinds of greed; a man's life does not consist in the abundance of his possessions" (Luke 12:15). "No servant can serve two masters. Either he will hate the one and love the other, or he will be devoted to the one and despise the other. You cannot serve both God and Money. The Pharisees, who loved money, heard all this and were sneering at Jesus. He said to them, 'You are the ones who justify yourselves in the eyes of men, but God knows your hearts. What is highly valued among men is detestable in God's sight'" (Luke 16:13–15).

To the rich young man who asked what he must do "to get eternal life," Jesus said, "If you want to be perfect, go, sell your possessions and give to the poor, and you will have treasure in heaven. Then come, follow me" (Matthew 19:21). This is a tall order for most of us; none of us comes close to perfection whatever our good intentions. After the rich man departed, Jesus turned to his disciples and said with compassion, "I tell you the truth, it is hard for a rich man to enter the kingdom of heaven. Again I tell you, it is easier for a camel to go through the eye of a needle than for a rich man to enter the kingdom of God" (Matthew 19:23–24; Mark 10:25).

I am not a theologian and would never second-guess Jesus' words, but I think what Jesus is saying is that the pursuit of wealth is seductive. I don't believe there is anything sinful about a nice house or decent clothes in themselves. It's just that possessions and material comforts can become powerful distractions from our true calling to "seek first the kingdom of God." When we are transformed by the power of God's love, our priorities change, and we choose to share our relative abundance with those in need.

Whatever else can be said about Jesus, he clearly was not complacent. When we hear of the passion of Christ, most of us think of Jesus' suffering on the cross. Less recognized is Jesus' passion in his daily life and teachings. I've always felt uncomfortable and misled with the description of Jesus as "meek and mild." He overthrew tables in the temple where vendors profited from the sale of sacrificial animals and money changing. He often found himself in the thick of controversy, like when he was asked to judge the woman caught in adultery (John 8:2–11). He denounced religious leaders with strong and derogatory language, "Woe to you, teachers of the law and Pharisees, you hypocrites . . . you snakes, you brood of vipers!" (Matthew 23:23, 33). There's no question that Jesus was outspoken and controversial, often shocking his listeners, including his disciples.

What in our lives are we truly passionate about? Is our faith on the back burner, awaiting some adverse event to activate it and move it front and center? Do we really have so little time that we cannot go for a walk in the woods in a quiet place where we can feel God's presence? Or share our frustration, pain, disappointment, and heartache with a God who loves us? Or rail at God for being cloaked in mystery, when we would prefer dramatic miracles? The point is that we are not to be passive or apathetic about seeking God and serving others. Indifference is not the way of Jesus.

CHAPTER 8

Worry, Joy, and Gratitude

FEAR AND WORRY ARE common emotions affecting the human psyche. Jesus clearly understood the prevalence of these emotions: by one count he said "fear not" or "do not be afraid" some fifty-seven times in the Gospels. Fear is built into our primitive brain-stem or "lizard brain," which helped humans to survive predators and other threats over the millennia. We have a tendency to fear and distrust outsiders who are of different racial or ethnic heritage, or who speak a foreign language, or who practice a faith we don't understand. Authoritarian leaders sometimes play on fears and worries to rally support for their cause.

But we are endowed not just with a reptilian brain but also with a frontal cortex that is able to reason with complexity. We can replace our knee-jerk fear with curiosity for those who look, think, and act differently than we do. We can seek to understand their heritage and customs. We can build relationships with people with whom we disagree and try to find common ground. In America a more inquisitive and accepting attitude would go a long way to breaking down barriers between ethnic and racial groups, urban and rural residents, those who live in the heartland compared to coastal states, and conservatives and progressives. In addition to our brains, we have hearts and souls, which connect us to others on a deeper, spiritual level.

Jesus declared, "Do not worry about your life, what you will eat or drink; or about your body, what you will wear. Is not life more

SPIRITUALITY & SOCIAL ACTION

important than food, and the body more important than clothes? Look at the birds of the air; they do not sow or reap or store away in barns, and yet your heavenly father feeds them. Are you not much more valuable than they? Who of you by worrying can add a single hour to his life? And why do you worry about clothes? See how the lilies of the field grow. They do not labor or spin. Yet I tell you that not even Solomon in all his splendor was dressed like one of these" (Matthew 6:25–29).

We humans seem to worry about everything, large and small: whether we will get our work done, whether we will regain our health, whether our children will be safe, whether we can afford to pay our bills, whether we will be late for a meeting, what we will have for dinner, etc. When I have an early morning flight to catch, I sometimes wake up repeatedly during the night, worried that I may have overslept my alarm.

We may not be able to turn off the worry button at all times, but we are called to live in a place of gratitude, giving thanks to God for our abundant blessings. Jesus explained, "I have said these things to you that you may have peace. In the world you will have tribulation. But take heart, I have overcome the world" (John 16:33). Whatever issues are going on in our lives, we are told to bring them to God in prayer, where we may find peace beyond all human understanding.

Christianity builds on a strong Jewish tradition of lament and thanksgiving, of sorrow and joy. Writers of the psalms go from the depths of despair to the heights of gratitude and praise:

> For troubles without number surround me;
> my sins have overtaken me, and I cannot see.
> They are more than the hairs of my head,
> and my heart fails within me. (Psalm 40:12)
> Come let us sing for joy to the Lord,
> let us shout aloud to the Rock of our salvation.
> Let us come before him with thanksgiving
> and extol him with music and song. (Psalm 95:1–2)

We are called to lay our cares at the feet of Jesus and allow God's healing presence to fill our being. Although I cited the following quote in chapter 2, it bears repeating here: "Come to me, all you who are weary and burdened, and I will give you rest. Take my yoke upon you and learn from me, for I am gentle and humble in heart, and you will find rest for your souls. For my yoke is easy and my burden is light" (Matthew 11:28–30).

When we yoke ourselves to the Lord, our burdens, stress, and worries become lighter. No longer do we feel that everything is our responsibility, but rather that our lives are a shared responsibility. We begin to understand that we can be part of the healing process, as God's spirit works through us. Paul says, "Therefore, if anyone is in Christ, he is a new creation, the old has gone, the new has come" (2 Corinthians 5:17).

All of us may get preoccupied with worry and sorrow, or become burned out with work and responsibilities. It seems we forget that "Jesus was full of joy through the Holy Spirit" (Luke 10:21). God wants us to enjoy life and relish God's abundance. We need to keep our eyes open not just to suffering, but also to joy, laugher, and play. They are expressions of God's love, and they feed our soul.

French philosopher and Jesuit priest Pierre Teilhard de Chardin said, "Joy is the infallible sign of the presence of God." Joy, hope, and love are all gifts from God. Is it appropriate to experience joy when there is so much suffering, sorrow, and despair in the world? It seems that joy is a way of bearing witness to God and a way of bringing light amidst the darkness. Joy is a zest for life that delights and celebrates the goodness of God. Jesus told his disciples, "As the Father has loved me, so have I loved you. Now remain in my love. If you obey my commands, you will remain in my love, just as I have obeyed my Father's commands and remain in his love. I have told you this so that my joy may be in you and your joy may be complete" (John 15:9–11).

Paul wrote, "Rejoice in the Lord always. I will say it again: Rejoice! Let your gentleness be evident to all. The Lord is near. Do not be anxious about anything, but in everything, by prayer and petition, with thanksgiving, present your requests to God. And the peace of God, which transcends all understanding, will guard your hearts and your minds in Christ Jesus" (Philippians 4:4–7).

We all know that our circumstances can change in an instant. One time I was bicycling at over forty-five miles per hour down a steep paved road from Anthony Lake in the Blue Mountains of eastern Oregon. I had been taking the descent casually, sitting up high in the saddle, enjoying the breeze, and treating my bike like a fun toy. Suddenly I noticed gravel on the asphalt, kicked up by vehicles that had driven too close to the unpaved shoulder. The presence of gravel changed everything and made the ride potentially treacherous. I grasped the drop bars and adjusted to a nearly horizontal position on the bike. Keeping my weight low and tight on the pedals and handlebar, I slowed my speed and made a few small zigzags to be sure that the bike was responsive to my slightest touch. In an instant I was one with the bike, a single entity gliding joyfully and safely down the mountain. I felt far more prepared for what the bike and I encountered on the road.

This may seem like a frivolous example, but being vulnerable, it hardly seemed innocuous at the time. Each of us has lived through difficult times in our lives; I have had my share of disappointments, frustrations, and pain. But we are not to dwell in the depths of darkness, but to take what corrective measures we can, and come out the other side into the light. We are to internalize God's abundant love and compassion and then to joyfully serve those who are hurting more than we. God wants us to flourish, to be fully alive, and to engage in the world.

Imagine what it can be like to be a part of God's plan for humanity, as much as we can understand it. It changes our perspective on everything. To effect real change, it needs to start within ourselves, daring to live the life that God intends for us. Frankly this is not an easy task; it takes effort and discipline on our part to understand and accept God's role for us. Richard Rohr states, "God wants useable instruments who will carry the mystery, the weight of glory and the burden of sin simultaneously, who can bear the darkness and the light, who can hold the paradox of incarnation—flesh and spirit, human and divine, joy and suffering, at the same time, just as Jesus did."[1]

A missionary in Peru starts his day, "Lord, do not allow us to become too comfortable." We are often most effective when we are

---

1. Rohr, *Things Hidden*, 35–36.

living outside our comfort zone, depending on God for guidance and strength. The spirit of God lives within each of us, inviting us to access God's grace and truth, and to share God's love with those we encounter. "For out of the overflow of the heart, the mouth speaks" (Matthew 12:34).

If we live our lives for God, we are filled with gratitude for our abundant blessings. We are no longer afraid and protective and self-absorbed, but are freed to trust in God. David, the shepherd boy who became king, clearly felt at one with God:

> Even though I walk through the valley of the shadow of death,
> I will fear no evil, for you are with me;
> Your rod and your staff, they comfort me . . .
> Surely goodness and love will follow me all the days of my life,
> And I will dwell in the house of the Lord forever." (Psalm 23:4, 6)

Why do we settle for the outward trappings of religion with its dogma, rituals, and even guilt trips, when we are offered so much more, namely, a direct experience of God? That's not to knock organized religion; it's just that our religious traditions often miss the mark of deepening our faith and inviting us into a closer relationship with God. Sometimes religion gets so convoluted that we can't see the forest for the trees, the Holy One for the holidays, the Messiah for the meetings.

We have the privilege of partnering with God to bring God's kingdom to Earth. Does this seem too good to be true—that we can actually play a part in God's plan? Paul wrote passionately about living a God-centered life: "Therefore as God's chosen people, holy and dearly loved, clothe yourselves with compassion, kindness, humility, gentleness and patience. Bear with each other and forgive whatever grievances you may have against one another. Forgive as the Lord forgave you. And over all these virtues, put on love, which binds them all together in perfect unity" (Colossians 3:12–14).

It is not an easy path to live our life for God rather than for ourselves. It means becoming vulnerable, exposed, and willing to share in the suffering of others. Rather than arrogantly declaring we are "self-made" men and women, we choose the way of humility and reliance on God. The apostle Paul reminds us that meaningful encounters with God result in the "fruits of the Spirit: love, joy, peace, patience, kindness, goodness, trustfulness, gentleness and self-control" (Galatians 5:22). This is what it means to walk in the footsteps of Jesus.

And what are we to do with these fruits? The answer is to give them away as fast as we can to anyone who can use them. We come from a place of abundance and are to respond to the needs and hurts of others with love, patience, and compassion. This is our true self, the part of us that is actually divine breath, just passing through us like a relay station. It is also the part of us that lives forever.

Jesus taught that we must deny our old selves, our ego, all the things we think are so important to our identity. "If anyone would come after me, he must deny himself and take up his cross and follow me. For whoever wants to save his life will lose it, but whoever loses his life for me will find it" (Matthew 16:24–25; Mark 8:34–35). The cross symbolizes discipleship, faith, sacrifice, and compassion. We are to live the life to which God calls us with humility, grace, and faithfulness. Leaving behind the pettiness of our former selves, we cross the threshold into God's kingdom, where values and priorities are so different. The good news is that our change of heart and the new orientation of our lives brings us into God's abundance. We are freed, liberated, and given new life by the grace of God.

CHAPTER 9

Prayer and Meditation

PRAYER IS AN ACT of communication with God. We usually think of prayer as a means of praising God, or petitioning God to help us cope with difficulties, or interceding for others in their time of need. Prayer is often a request for God to intervene, to provide help, or to fix a perceived problem. It may be very personal or global in intent. We may pray fervently to get us through our time of trouble, only to put our faith aside until we are confronted with the next crisis.

We think of prayer as words, a request to God for what is on our hearts. But words are optional, and prayer is also waiting patiently and listening for God's word through meditation. Prayer stands at the place where God and humans meet. Through prayer we connect with God and feel God's presence, however tenuous that may seem. As Rev. Beth Neel, copastor of Westminster Presbyterian Church in Portland, said in a sermon, "Just the desire for prayer, our seeking to reach out to God, is more important than what we ask for."

Paul writes, "We do not know what we ought to pray for, but the Spirit himself intercedes for us with groans that words cannot express" (Romans 8:26). We are not born knowing how to pray. Even Jesus' disciples asked him to teach them how to pray. His response, commonly known as the Lord's Prayer and translated in the New Zealand Maori Anglican liturgy, is as follows:

Eternal Spirit,
Earth-maker, Pain bearer, Life-giver,
Source of all that is and that shall be,
Father and Mother of us all,
Loving God, in whom is heaven:

The hallowing of your name echo through the universe;
The way of your justice be followed by the peoples of the world;
Your heavenly will be done by all created beings;
Your commonwealth of peace and freedom
sustain our hope and come on earth.

With the bread we need for today, feed us.
In the hurts we absorb from one another, forgive us.
In times of temptation and test, strengthen us.
From trial too great to endure, spare us.
From the grip of all that is evil, free us.
For you reign in the glory of the power that is love,
now and forever. Amen.

At first, prayer may seem a bit awkward, like taking up a new sport or new activity that requires training and practice. None of us were fluid and skillful when we first tried swimming or reading, but over time we developed more competence. Eventually such activities became a natural and integral part of our skill set. So too, prayer is an opportunity to hone our spiritual skills, as we seek to draw closer to God. We are all apprentices in God's kingdom, and God accepts us all, wherever we may be on our spiritual path.

Prayer should be a pleasure, not a burden. Think of when you were a young child and climbed into the lap of your grandmother or grandfather to hear a story, and you felt loved and nurtured. This feeling is not unlike the trust of sitting quietly and expectantly in the presence of God, whom we may think of by the more intimate name of Abba, which means "Father" or "Daddy" in Greek.

God ultimately desires a relationship with each of us and waits to hear from us through our prayers. Prayer allows us to connect with God's love, compassion, patience, and grace. As we listen quietly with humility and openness, we will draw closer to God and our sense of separateness begins to dissolve. Prayer and meditation become our lifeline to God. Over time this practice may become such an integral part of our daily routine that it is incorporated into most everything we do.

None of us appreciates when someone talks *at* us in a one-way monologue. Conversations are meant to have dialogue between individuals. Similarly, prayer can be a two-way communication between Creator and created, a bridge between our spiritual self and God. Prayer is not so much about talking; it is more a shift in consciousness into the spiritual dimension to tune in to God's will and purpose. Author and lecturer Philip Yancey writes, "What I learn from spending time with God better equips me to discern what God wants to do on earth, as well as my role in that plan . . . Persistent prayer changes me by helping me to see the world, and my life, through God's eyes."[1] Yancey goes on, "During the day thoughts and impressions come to mind that stem directly from my prayers. I am far more likely to view events that occur and people I encounter from God's point of view."[2]

Personally, I have found tremendous help through centering prayer. For the purposes of this book, "centering prayer," "contemplative prayer," "contemplation," and "meditation" are used interchangeably. For nuances in these terms and a deeper understanding of centering prayer, you may want to consult the writings of Thomas Merton, Thomas Keating, and Richard Rohr in the bibliography. Other terms include "guidance," as used by my grandmother, whom we knew as "Precious," and "quiet time," my father's term for meditation each morning.

Centering prayer requires that we withdraw from the noise and busyness of our lives and quietly open ourselves to the presence of God. When we love someone, we choose to spend time with our beloved. Centering prayer is choosing to spend time with God in quiet and without distractions. This type of meditation moves beyond words to awareness and consciousness. In a world filled with distractions and demands, it may not be easy to find a quiet time and place to connect with God. It usually means getting up a bit

1. Yancey, *Prayer*, 152.
2. Yancey, *Prayer*, 162.

earlier each morning and finding a quiet space away from family and interruptions.

By relaxing our bodies and quieting the chatter of our minds, we allow our hearts to be sensitive to the spiritual dimension, which at first we may only vaguely sense. Contemplation is surrendering our minds and our egos and allowing ourselves to wait quietly in the presence of God, gradually drawing closer to the spiritual dynamic going on just out of sight.

The essence of who I am doesn't come from my body, or intellect, or emotions. It comes from deep in my being, a place that may be referred to as the soul. It is there that I tap into a power of love and compassion, what I believe is the indwelling presence of God. As Jesus said, "The kingdom of God is within you" (Luke 17:21). Psalm 46:11 declares, "Be still and know that I am God." We are invited to open ourselves to God's presence, which surrounds, embraces, and fills us.

What are some of the methods of practicing centering prayer? In a comfortable, relaxed posture, with eyes closed, we need to free our minds of any thoughts by gently, effortlessly letting them go. Our biggest obstacle to accessing God's presence is our mind, which often wants to ruminate on the past or make plans for the future. During meditation the activity of the mind is like static; it creates a background buzz that interferes with being in the present moment. In reality my thoughts are usually petty and repetitive; so few of them are original and creative. Thinking will dominate my waking hours if I don't intentionally choose to turn it off during meditation. As Episcopal priest Cynthia Bourgeault said at a conference, "With centering prayer intention is everything—the intention to be open, to be available to God. The power of intention will call you back from distractions."

If clearing the mind is hard to do, using a mantra may be helpful, a phrase like "Into your hands," or "In your holy presence," or "I love you, God," or "O, Holy One." Some prefer to quote Scripture, such as, "Be at rest once more, O my soul, for the Lord has been good to you" (Psalm 116:7). Others recite the Jesus Prayer, "Lord Jesus Christ, Son of God, have mercy on me, a sinner," a prayer rooted in the Eastern Orthodox tradition. We shouldn't force the process of clearing our mind, but rather be gentle on ourselves, particularly at first, as this practice becomes easier with time. Richard Rohr talks about putting our thoughts on a little boat and letting the current gently float them away.

By tuning out the distractions of the mind, we are able to access a dimension that goes well beyond thought. We are in the present moment where we can draw closer to the unfathomable dimension of the Creator. While in centering prayer, the veil between God and us becomes thinner and more porous. In the words of Thomas Keating, "We tend to live in the world of our thoughts and emotions which impose themselves and buffet us relentlessly. But beyond our thinking and emotional experience is the deeper reality of the spiritual level of our being. This is a place of peace and joy where we connect with the divine presence. It is another way of knowing reality that is unlike ordinary psychological awareness."[3]

During a daily time of centering prayer, two things become evident. First, being in God's presence brings peace. Worries and regrets seem petty and no longer have the same relevance when compared to being close to God. The past is done, and there is little fear of the future. Connecting with God, however tenuous it may seem, is what truly matters. Second, each of us is incredibly blessed. Jesus said, "I have come that they may have life, and have it to the full" (John 10:10). Jesus came to show us the heart of God, and through Jesus' teachings and actions, we learn that God is not distant and vengeful, but rather is loving, compassionate, and forgiving. When we choose to spend time in God's presence, we are transformed by the grace of God.

Trappist monk Thomas Merton described the experience this way: "Contemplation is life itself, fully awake, fully active, fully aware that it is alive. It is spiritual wonder. It is spontaneous awe at the sacredness of life, of being. It is gratitude for life, for awareness, and for being. It is a vivid realization of the fact that life and being in us proceed from an invisible, transcendent, and infinitely abundant Source. Contemplation is, above all, awareness of the reality of that Source. It knows the source, obscurely, inexplicably, but with a

3. Keating, Daily Reader, 174.

certitude that goes beyond reason and beyond simple faith . . . It is a more profound depth of faith, a knowledge too deep to be grasped in images, in words, or even in clear concepts."[4]

At it's best, centering prayer fills us with God's blessings. Whatever our circumstances, we have a sense of abundance and wholeness. God breathes new life into us, and we are replenished and filled with God's love. Blessings well up from within and spill over into the lives of others. We become more patient and compassionate beings, instruments of God's peace. The epistle of James tells us, "Come near to God and he will come near you" (James 4:8).

At it's worst, centering prayer is frustrating, with distractions from our mind, or annoying intrusions from outside. God may seem distant and aloof. Perhaps the day's agenda is dominating our thoughts, or we are consumed with anxieties and worries. But even when the connection is poor or nonexistent, waiting patiently on the Lord is nearly always of value. It quiets the mind, reduces anxieties, and opens the door to God's peace.

C. S. Lewis wrote, "God designed the human machine to run on Himself. He Himself is the fuel our spirits were designed to burn, or the food our spirits were designed to feed on. There is no other."[5] Without centering prayer, if I just run on autopilot, I lack patience and compassion. I feel out of sorts all day, not really tuned into other people and their needs, and likely to miss opportunities to make a difference in their lives.

I could give many examples of how I fail miserably to do God's will on a regular basis, but one that comes to mind occurred early last December. I was heading downtown to do Christmas shopping for my out-of-town relatives. I was a man on a mission, totally focused on purchasing and mailing gifts before the Christmas rush. Half a block from Powell's bookstore, I passed an elderly and disfigured woman in a wheelchair on the sidewalk, and she looked up at me plaintively and spoke in a nearly inaudible whisper, "Please, sir, can you help?" I'm ashamed to admit that I didn't respond but hurried by, saying to myself that I would stop to help

4. Merton, *Choosing to Love the World*, 47
5. Lewis, *Mere Christianity*, 124

her on my way back. Needless to say, the woman was gone when I emerged from Powell's.

Once again I had totally failed the Good Samaritan test. Can you imagine Jesus ignoring the blind Bartimaeus, or the lame beggars, or the lepers who called out to him as he passed by? Hardly. We ourselves may not have the ability to cure people of their illnesses, but we can take the time to hear their plight and do what we can to help, even if that is just a sympathetic ear and a few dollars.

Centering prayer keeps us attuned to God's priorities and able to respond to the needs around us. It is most effective as an ongoing, daily encounter, since the connection doesn't carry over very well from one day to the next. An analogy is how our muscles, ligaments, and joints often stiffen up overnight and need to be stretched each morning. So too, my faith has to be stretched, my priorities reset, and my soul replenished with divine love on a daily basis.

Centering prayer is a time to reorient our lives in alignment with God's will. By coming close to the Almighty, we tap into a reservoir of God's love, healing, and wholeness. We can be the visible sign of an invisible God. We may be the only evidence of God's existence that someone will see or know that day. For Christians our model is Jesus, who prayed frequently, was always connected to God, and was fully engaged with people.

Personally, I need to open myself to God's presence for about twenty minutes each morning to receive my daily infusion of grace. Since we live in a busy and noisy society, full of cell phones, computers, TVs, and other distractions and interruptions, I have found the best time for me is first thing in the morning. Having a special and "holy" place for centering prayer is important—a chair or window seat where I can relax in stillness and feel God's presence. In doing centering prayer with Richard Rohr at Center for Action and Contemplation in Albuquerque, we sat on the floor with our backs against a wall. Alternatively, some people have a favorite site in the woods because they feel closer God's presence in nature. Wherever the location, we should feel a great sense of peace, belonging, and oneness with God's spirit.

When I have been in God's presence, I live my life differently, expecting to find God in nearly all situations. My radar is turned on, and I begin to experience God through nature and in everyday encounters with people.

I want to conclude this discussion of centering prayer by looking at ten reasons why it is a counterintuitive concept and practice in today's world:

1. We are not accustomed to silence. Our daily lives are bombarded with distractions, including social media, news and advertising. Our senses are continually stimulated. Sitting quietly seems unnatural and foreign to us.

2. We tend to live more in our heads than in our hearts. We are rational beings, products of the enlightenment and dependent on our intellect. It is difficult for us to turn our minds off, let our thoughts go, and just *be* in an unstructured space.

3. We find it incomprehensible that God would actually want to spend time with us. We can't grasp that God desires this one-on-one relationship more than anything—in fact, it is the primary reason we were created.

4. We want certitude in our faith, to be sure that we are on the right path. What we experience in centering prayer is nebulous and uncertain, filled with unknowing more than knowing. Why doesn't God present us with a burning bush or a miracle so that we can be sure?

5. We like to be in control. After all, we Americans think of ourselves as self-made men and women, independent-minded and self-sufficient. Dependence on God flies in the face of American rugged individualism and self-reliance.

6. By contrast, centering prayer is choosing to rest in the lap of Abba, where we feel nurtured and loved. It is turning over control to God, a feeling of letting go.

7. Some people live in fear: fear of financial insecurity, fear of losing a job or spouse, fear of what others may think of them, fear of people who are different, etc. They build walls to protect themselves and their privileged way of life. Walls are the antithesis of connection, inclusiveness, and oneness with God and humanity.

8. To practice meditation, we need to be fully present and in touch with our feelings. If we take little time for self-examination and self-reflection, we are less likely to be able to open ourselves to the presence of God.

9. Our insecure egos trap us into thinking we need to look good, be smart, act superior, and garner the esteem of our peers. Connecting with God's spirit takes us in the opposite direction of humility and selflessness, where what we are is who we are in God.

10. Finally, centering prayer or meditation typically is not preached from the pulpit. But in reality, it is widely practiced by Christians who seek a closer relationship with God and a deeper experience of faith. To distill it down to its essence, it is quietly waiting in the presence of God.

Regarding spiritual growth and centering prayer, Thomas Keating wrote, "It's a process, dear friends, and the taste that we have of God can continue to develop into ever deeper levels of intimacy that are absolutely inconceivable to us in the beginning—beyond anything, as Paul says, we could imagine or dream of is the closeness of God's presence."[6]

6. Keating, *Daily Reader*, 261.

CHAPTER 10

Faith and Doubt

I BELIEVE GOD LISTENS to our petitions and responds to our prayers, although not necessarily in the time frame that we have in mind and often not in the way we might expect. To give an example, a decade ago I was developing a global health course at Oregon Health & Science University, and was on the verge of burnout, planning the course curriculum, scheduling speakers, registering students, applying for continuing medical education credits, managing course finances, and many other tasks. The responsibilities and deadlines were weighing me down to the point that I felt depleted of energy and nearly immobilized.

I reserved a room at the Shalom Center in Mt. Angel, Oregon, for a solo retreat over the weekend. The grounds are beautiful, they have a lovely modern chapel, and meals are served with the nuns in the dining hall. I knew my engine was sputtering, and I was driving on fumes. I prayed that God would take the pressure and stress off my shoulders. Alone in my room, I opened my Bible to the Psalms and found I was in good company:

> "I am poor and needy;
> may the Lord think of me.
> You are my help and my deliverer
> O my God, do not delay." (Psalm 40:17)

"Be still before the Lord and wait patiently for him."
(Psalm 37:17)

"I waited patiently for the Lord;
he turned to me and heard my cry.
He lifted me out of the slimy pit;
He set my feet on a rock." (Psalm 40:1–2)

How God responded to my supplications was unforeseen and remarkable. That weekend I didn't resolve a single issue with the global health course that seemed so overwhelming to me. But I began to write a speech that I was scheduled to give the following weekend at Peace Plaza in Salem. I opened my laptop, and the ideas and words came tumbling out onto the screen. I wasn't aware that I was stressing over this additional commitment, but once I had written the speech, I felt a sense of immense peace and gratitude. The Lord works in strange and mysterious ways and answered my prayer in a manner I never expected. It was the gift I needed to move on with new energy, feeling embraced and supported by the Lord. I came home from the weekend with renewed spirit and hope.

Another example: I was on a team of volunteers working at Gimbie Hospital in eastern Ethiopia in 2009. We arrived to find that our dorm was still under construction. A heavy layer of concrete dust covered the bed and everything else in the small room. The plumbing didn't work, and the only window was a narrow slit with bars across it. When I went to close the steel door to the room, it clanged shut, locking me in the room because my room key didn't fit the lock. Since I tend to be claustrophobic, this situation brought on a near panic attack. I had no choice but to spend the night in the room and wait to summon help in the morning. I prayed much of the night, and felt God's presence and peace, and eventually fell asleep for a few hours. When I heard other team members stirring in the morning, they were able to open the door from the corridor and let me out of my "prison cell."

My encounter in a foreign land was unnerving but short-lived. I reminded myself that hardship and failure, as tough as they may be, can be great learning tools and may bring us into closer relationship with God. Paul wrote to the Corinthians, "We are hard-pressed on every side, yet not crushed; we are perplexed, but not in despair; persecuted, but not forsaken; struck down, but not destroyed" (2 Corinthians 4:8–9). The Psalms are full of supplication to God during dark and challenging times. When David was fleeing the army of King Saul, he wrote, "The Lord is my light and my salvation—whom shall I fear? The Lord is the stronghold of my life—of whom shall I be afraid? . . . For in the day of trouble he will keep me safe in his dwelling; he will hide me in the shelter of his tabernacle and set me high upon a rock" (Psalm 27:1, 5).

Our goal should be to seek out God not only in times of stress or crisis, but also in the routines of life. We live in a society where it is so easy to get distracted by cell phones, advertising, media, and entertainment. These intrusions shut us down from a sense of God's presence. When we have an ongoing awareness of God and expect to find God in each encounter, we begin to see the world in a new light, perhaps as God sees it. It has been said that sin is anything that cuts us off from God. How do we know when we have strayed from God's will? We just have to look at our motives—are they self-serving, intended to enhance our own self-image, or are they rooted in compassion and humility?

What does God ask of us? I don't pretend to know God's intentions, but it seems that what God wants most is to have an ongoing relationship with us. Our faithfulness to God, not our goodness, is what is important. Both the Old and New Testaments say to "Love the Lord, your God, with all your heart, with all your soul, with all your mind, and with all your strength" (Deuteronomy 6:5; Levitiucs 19:18; Luke 10:27). To love God with this intensity requires humility and gratitude, faith and tenacity. We are to offer our entire being to God, and such a commitment takes a major leap of faith.

Fortunately, God is patient with us. The process has been incremental for me, gradually releasing my own willfulness and asking for God's direction. As I wait quietly on the Lord, I may discern God's will, which often includes ideas that would never occur to me on my own . . . like writing a book on spirituality and social action! It has become apparent that God is not just out there, but is a living presence within each of us. This may not be evident at first, but it is certainly fundamental to Jesus' teachings: "Streams of living water will flow from within" (John 7:38). God is an indwelling presence, waiting to share an abundance of love with each of us.

How can we live both in the world and in God's realm at the same time? We have to struggle with this paradox. The world wants to suck us into its vortex of materialism, power, and desire for recognition and success. By contrast, God calls us to the deep well of compassion and love, that part of us we sometimes refer to as the soul. When we feel blessed and trust in God, we can more easily let go of our superficial distractions and ego.

And what is the role of Jesus in this relationship with God? Jesus is the visible, tangible, historic, and living presence of God. Jesus said, "I am in the Father and the Father is in me. The words I say to you are not just my own. Rather it is the Father, living in me, who is doing His work" (John 14:10). And who are the seekers of a spiritual way? "You are a chosen people, a royal priesthood, a holy nation, a people belonging to God, that you may declare the praises of him who called you out of darkness into his wonderful light" (1 Peter 2:9–11). This priesthood of believers is not an exclusive club, but rather a ragtag, motley group of sinners seeking to do God's will.

Will we face doubt along the way? Of course; faith and doubt go hand in hand. Even John the Baptist, who had staked his prophetic message of repentance on the Messiah, and had witnessed the spirit of God descending on Jesus like a dove, had doubts. Jesus was not acting the way John expected the Messiah to act. After all, Jesus consorted with outcasts and sinners, and enjoyed eating and drinking at the homes of rich people—hardly the diet of "locusts and honey" of John and his disciples. From prison, John sent his disciples to question Jesus, "Are you the one who was to come (the Messiah) or should we expect someone else?" (Matthew 11:3). Jesus' reply was unequivocal: "Go back and report to John what you hear and see: The blind receive sight, the lame walk, those who have leprosy are cured, the deaf hear, the dead are raised, and the good news is preached to the poor" (Matthew 11:4–5).

If even John the Baptist had doubts, it gives us license to have doubts too. Faith is a choice we make based on our experience. It forces us to move beyond the limitations of our rational mind, our culture, and our early religious upbringing. Faith invites us to trust our lives to God and risk everything. If God were 100 percent provable, it would not be faith, but a scientific reality. We would be able to shrug off God, much like we take gravity for granted. Gone would be the need to invest time and energy to seek divine truth. There would be little reason for Jesus' intervention in the world to reveal the nature of God. If God is a certainty, our search for meaning becomes a done deal, like reading the conclusion of a mystery story first to see how it all comes out. How boring is that? And what incentive would there be to explore the mystery of God?

Sometimes the Bible is difficult to understand or just doesn't make much sense. We need to wrestle and struggle with faith, like Jacob wrestling with an angel of the Lord in Genesis 32:22–30. Rob Bell, pastor of Mars Hill Church in Grandville, Michigan, writes, "The ultimate display of our respect for the sacred words of God is that we are willing to wade in and struggle with the text—the good parts, the hard-to-understand parts, the parts we wish weren't there ... [Jacob] struggles, and it is exhausting and tiring, and in the end his hip is injured. It hurts. And he walks away limping. Because when you wrestle with the text, you walk away limping. And some people have no limp, because they haven't wrestled. The ones limping have had an experience with the Living God."[1]

Lutheran pastor and theologian Dietrich Bonhoeffer spent two years in a Nazi prison in World War II, weathering the struggles that his faith demanded. He understood his calling as costly discipleship, and ended up paying for his beliefs with his life at age thirty-nine. Following our calling may entail suffering and sacrifice.

1. Bell, *Velvet Elvis*, 68–69.

CHAPTER 11

Jesus and Social Justice

JESUS SAID, "THE SON of Man did not come to be served, but to serve" (Matthew 20:28; Mark 10:45). Jesus ministered to the outcasts of Palestine, e.g., lepers, psychotics (demon possessed), the blind, deaf, and lame, and many others who lived on the margins of society. He served not only Jews but also Romans, Samaritans, Canaanites, and Gerasenes.

As discussed in chapter 8, Jesus taught, "If anyone would come after me, he must deny himself and take up his cross and follow me" (Matthew 16:24). In this day to deny ourselves is countercultural; we want the best for ourselves and our children. Jesus calls us to live more simply and to share what we have. He says we should follow him where he resides, namely with the poor and marginalized. *Christianity is not just a way of believing, but a way of living.* Those of us who are followers of Jesus are called to reach out to the poor, the sick, the homeless, the vulnerable, and all those who are not at the table for whatever reason.

Our innate tendency is to move away from things that make us uncomfortable, but Jesus teaches us to move toward suffering. If we always live within our comfort zone, we are missing the point, because the needy don't live on our street, nor do they frequent the same churches, stores, and social gatherings that we enjoy. They are likely to be found in a tent under an overpass, or standing in line at a soup kitchen, or waiting on a street corner for a day labor job, or holding up a cardboard sign at an intersection. We shouldn't be surprised if they don't look and smell like we do, despite all of us being God's children. If we contribute to an organization that is feeding the hungry, or serve meals to the needy ourselves, we are on the right path. But if we take the time to get to know those who are struggling and listen to their stories, we are performing the work of Jesus. When Jesus says "love your neighbor as yourself," he is talking about a much greater commitment than just writing a check to charity.

Jesus addresses wealth and poverty more than heaven or hell. His teachings are laced with the importance of caring for orphans, widows, foreigners, the poor, and the needy. Jesus never asked questions of worthiness of those he served, but rather he was ready to include, forgive and accept everyone in need. The Gospel of Luke quotes Jesus as saying, "Give, and it will be given to you. A good measure, pressed down, shaken together and running over, will be poured into your lap. For with the measure you use, it will be measured to you" (Luke 6:38). Conversely, Proverbs says, "If a man shuts his ears to the cry of the poor, he too will cry out and not be heard" (Proverbs 21:13).

Jesus' greatest scorn was reserved for the scribes and Pharisees, who lived by the letter, if not the spirit, of the law. Jesus called the Pharisees "hypocrites" and a "brood of vipers." He admonished them, "You clean the outside of the cup and dish, but inside they are full of greed and self-indulgence. Blind Pharisee! First clean the inside of the cup and dish, and then the outside also will be clean. Woe to you, teachers of the law and Pharisees, you hypocrites! You are like whitewashed tombs, which look beautiful on the outside but on the inside are full of dead men's bones and everything unclean. In the same way, on the outside you appear to people as righteous but on the inside you are full of hypocrisy and wickedness" (Matthew 23:25–28).

God wants us to live our lives not by lofty creeds and pious ideals, but with humility, caring, and service. We are to seek our place in God's design and trust God's purpose. Our calling is to love God and to serve God by ministering to the needs of others. We are to feel the pain and suffering of others and make it our own. How remarkable that God willingly uses us with all of our imperfections to carry out God's purpose!

Service is about sharing God's love, thereby enriching both the giver and the receiver. "Thy kingdom come on earth as it is in heaven" is not wishful thinking but an imperative for change. We must walk together with God's children and be sure that everyone gets to come to the table and has enough to eat. If the system is failing those who are most vulnerable, e.g., families living on the street, then we need to go upstream and see what needs to be done to fix the system.

Martin Luther King Jr. preached, "Jesus gave us a new norm of greatness. If you want to be important—wonderful; if you want to be recognized—wonderful; if you want to be great—wonderful. But recognize that he who is greatest among you shall be your servant. That's a new definition of greatness . . . It means that everybody can be great because everybody can serve. You don't have to have a college degree to serve. You don't have to make your subject and your verb agree to serve. You don't have to know about Plato and Aristotle to serve. You don't have to know Einstein's theory of relativity to serve. You don't have to know the second theory of thermodynamics in physics to serve. You only need a heart full of grace, a soul generated by love. And you can be that servant."[1]

When I look at a stranger, do I see them with harsh, judgmental eyes? Do I keep my distance because they look and speak differently than me? If they are people of color or handicapped or unattractive, do I let my position of privilege create a gulf between us? This is not the way of Jesus, who taught us to welcome the stranger. We are to look at others with soft eyes of compassion and look for the positive intent in every person. Evangelical leader Tony Campolo speaks about looking *into* a person, not *at*. We need to look into the face of a homeless person and try to connect to his/her inner humanity.

Forty years ago I was walking in downtown San Francisco when a homeless man approached me and asked, "Can you help me?" Being from a small city and unaccustomed to being accosted on the street, I remember looking right through him like he didn't exist, and I was unable to speak. In that brief encounter, it didn't

1. King, "Drum Major Instinct," sermon, February 4, 1968, in *I Have a Dream*, 189–90.

quite register that he was more than a generic homeless person; he was in fact a living being with real needs. He handled the encounter better than I did, saying with a shrug, "I guess not." I thought at the time, this clearly is not the way Jesus would have handled the situation. Jesus responded to everyone in need and had compassion for the poor, hungry, homeless, sick, and marginalized. Today, I keep a separate pouch in my wallet ("God's pouch") with small-denomination bills so that I can respond to needy strangers on the street without awkwardly fumbling through my wallet.

God extends infinite love and mercy to us, and this is how we are to treat ourselves and others. We first have to love ourselves before we can love others. Only when we view ourselves with compassionate, nonjudgmental eyes can we see others in the same light. We can't give to anyone else what we don't have within ourselves. The Dalai Lama teaches, "You begin by cherishing yourself. All religions teach that you must love yourself first. To cherish oneself is not easy. We are each of us a child of God. We must cherish the life we are given and cherish the life of others. Remember that we all want the same thing: to avoid suffering and find happiness."[2]

In 2017 I injured my right knee while leading a hike in Portland for out-of-town attendees of a public health conference. As a tour guide, I felt obligated to continue the hike over rough terrain in Forest Park, even though my knee was painful and swollen. In the following weeks and months, I needed to use a cane until I underwent surgery five months later. I admit that before this injury I had been a bit dismissive of people with canes as "cripples," lumped together with people with other physical disabilities. When I walked with a cane, I was one of them, and we shared a common bond. Today, I can relate to people with canes and crutches and see them with more compassionate, less judgmental eyes.

I have a favorite place on a window seat on Orcas Island where I like to meditate. Sometimes the mist creeps in and shrouds the bushes and trees and makes an island of the house where I sit. Like the soft mist, we need to be gentle, tolerant, and loving toward all we meet. Each person is a child of God, and each has his/her own

2. Dalai Lama, quoted from a talk at University of Portland, May 9, 2013.

story, including struggles, disappointments, and joys. We need to be ready with an encouraging word, a warm smile, and a humorous comment to lighten their day. New Thought spiritual leader Mary Manin Morrissey preaches, "Our capacity to love sets up a field of vibrations."[3] To extend the love of God to others is the natural flow of compassion from the heart.

As Christians, our calling goes beyond personal salvation to include carrying out the work of social justice and reconciliation, as demonstrated by the life and teachings of Jesus. For those of us who have grown up with white privilege, this means trying to understand the very different experience of growing up as an African-American with enduring racial prejudice. Or if we were born into the comforts of the middle class, we need to be able to relate to those who were born into poverty, where the odds against breaking out of poverty are formidable.

Jesus does not sugarcoat his message of what it means to be his follower. He says:

> But woe to you who are rich, for you have already received your comfort.
> Woe to you who are well fed now, for you will go hungry.
> Woe to you who laugh now, for you will mourn and weep.
> Woe to you when all men speak well of you, for that is how their fathers
> treated the false prophets. (Luke 6:24–26)

Do these admonitions make us feel uncomfortable? They should, and they do for me. These radical ideas are as hard to hear in the twenty-first century as they were at the time Jesus spoke them. We are called to share our good fortune and resources with those who are in need. If we are esteemed members of our community, we need a healthy dose of humility and concern for those at the bottom of the economic and social pyramid. Following Jesus is much more than seeking personal salvation; it is a higher calling to join him in the trenches of life where people are hurting the most.

---

3. Morrissey, quoted from a sermon at Living Enrichment Center, Wilsonville, Oregon.

CHAPTER 12

The Way of a Servant

THERE'S NO DENYING THE hurt and suffering in the world today. Man's inhumanity to man has been present throughout human history, but in recent years we have witnessed a cascade of revelations about the abuse of children, women, blacks, immigrants, Muslims, Jews, gays, transgender people, the homeless, and numerous other vulnerable populations. We can't combat all the evils of the world, but we can be a conduit for God's love and compassion to those who are hurting and needy.

Teacher and author Verna Dozier writes, "God has paid us the high compliment of calling us to be coworkers with our Creator."[1] When we offer ourselves to God, we in turn begin to offer compassion to others; this is God's transforming power. God's love is constant; it is we who choose to open or shut the door. We are not *whole* until we touch the *holy* and tap into God's infinite source of love. We begin to look for and anticipate opportunities where God can use us to reach out to the needs of others. Jesus makes it clear that we are not to favor the hierarchal system that gives power and prestige to the few at the top: "The first will be last, and the last will be first" (Matthew 20:16). God's kingdom favors the humble, not the arrogant, and calls out for justice for those who are vulnerable and marginalized. Those at the bottom need to be empowered with a voice equal to those who are privileged.

1. Dozier, *Dream of God*, 145.

Jesus gives us examples of how to be of service: "For I was hungry and you gave me something to eat. I was thirsty and you gave me something to drink. I was a stranger and you invited me in. I needed clothes and you clothed me. I was sick and you looked after me. I was in prison and you came to visit me . . . I tell you the truth, whatever you did for one of the least of these brothers of mine, you did for me" (Matthew 25:35, 40). Most of us know people who are lonely, or are sick, or going through tough times. Will we reach out to them with compassion and love in the spirit of Jesus?

In a speech at Western Michigan University on December 18, 1963, Dr. Martin Luther King Jr. reminded his audience, "All life is interrelated, that somehow we're caught in an inescapable network of mutuality tied in a single garment of destiny. Whatever affects one directly, affects all indirectly." Our calling is to show compassion and serve "the least of these," our brothers and sisters who are poor, homeless, hungry, sick, imprisoned, lonely, and marginalized.

At some point in our spiritual journey we find that Jesus' view becomes more important than our own narrow perspective. As we begin to see the world through the eyes of Jesus, we have greater compassion, both for ourselves and for others. We enjoy greater humility and charity, and are better able to connect with others who are hurting. Thomas Keating wrote, "The insight into Christ dwelling in every other person enables one to express charity toward others with greater spontaneity. Instead of seeing only someone's personality, race, nationality, gender, status, or characteristics (which you like or do not like), you see what is deepest—one's union or potential union with Christ. You also perceive everyone's desperate need of help. The transcendent potential of most people is still waiting to be realized, and this awakens a great sense of compassion."[2]

Jesus said, "My command is this: Love each other as I have loved you" (John 15:12). Jesus calls us to love fully and unconditionally. This is way beyond polite pleasantries like "Have a nice day." It is leading with our heart, being vulnerable, and connecting deeply with people. Our response may be, "That's fine for Jesus, but I'm not capable of loving that fully." On our own this is true, but

2. Keating, *Open Mind, Open Heart*, 103.

we are called to be a pass-through conduit of God's unending love. We don't initiate love; we just tap into the divine source in order to share it with others. Each of us can become an instrument of God's grace; the most ordinary encounters can be transformed into expressions of God's love.

Leading a life of faith is not easy; this is not la-la land and is not for the faint of heart. Stephen Mattson writes, "To survive the spiritual journey of Christianity, you must understand what you're getting into, because following Jesus will likely be harder than you imagine and more grueling than you've been told . . . Dedicating your life to Christ is radically different from how many pastors portray it, contradictory to how many Christians practice it, and incompatible with what many institutions claim it to be."[3]

Helping to build the kingdom of God can be messy and uncomfortable. At times we will see the hand of God transforming peoples lives; at other times we will encounter senseless tragedy, despair, failure, resentment, and hostility. In Acts 16 we read that Paul and his companions were beaten, flogged, and thrown into prison at Philippi. Yet when the going looked bleakest, shackled in a prison dungeon, Paul, Silas, and Timothy saw adversity as an opportunity, and continued to pray and sing hymns of praise. They felt secure in their faith and saw the prison as an opportunity to witness to other prisoners and the jailer. Discipleship is a privilege whatever the hardships.

Fortunately, we are not called to be all things to all people. We need to reflect upon our gifts and talents and where we can best fit into God's plan. For most of us this is not to be a pastor or missionary, but rather to impact our family, friends, neighbors, colleagues, and those who are poor and sick in our community. Opportunities to build the kingdom of God are all around us, if we but open our eyes and hearts to God's calling. And importantly, we are not to expect recognition and praise for our efforts. Jesus tells the story of a master and his servant, "Would he (the master) thank the servant because he (the servant) did what he was told to do? So you also, when you have done everything you were told to do, should say, 'We are unworthy servants; we have only done our duty'" (Luke 17:9–10).

3. Mattson, *Great Reckoning*, 83.

We need to recognize that we are not as effective if we try to go down this path of discipleship alone. We all need mentors and other believers to share the journey and encourage one another. For over five years, I mentored a young boy from a dysfunctional family, seeing him for a few hours once a week. But the agency that matched us had no mentor coaching and no opportunity for feedback over that extended period of time. The staff were good people who were vastly overextended and unable to provide mentoring and followup. I feel I would have been more effective if I had been able to check in periodically with both the agency personnel and other mentors to discuss what was working and what was not. Eventually the boy was adopted by a family in another city, his name was changed, and all of his family and friends (including me) were cut off from further contact. Now the boy has grown to be a man of twenty-two, and we have reconnected via Facebook. Sadly, the cycle of poverty is such a powerful vortex that thus far it has trapped him in unhealthy lifestyles and poor choices. I'm honestly not sure if I made a difference in his life. If there is hope, it is because he talks of completing his high school education and joining the Job Corps. In retrospect, I think I would have been more effective if I had had the opportunity to work under the guidance of a child development specialist and in collaboration with other mentors.

Christian discipleship takes personal commitment, as well as working together with other believers who share a common vision. We need the support of each other in our inevitable times of humiliation and failure. Wherever we are in our faith journey, we need mentors to guide and encourage us, while at the same time we may be able to serve as mentors for others. Seeking the kingdom of God is a bumpy road for fallible beings like us, but we will travel it more effectively if we travel together.

In August, 2012, I lost a good friend while biking in Montana. One moment he was fit and healthy and full of fun and life, and the next moment he had collapsed, dropped to the pavement, and was unresponsive to attempts to resuscitate him. I struggled mightily when I called his wife to explain what had happened, and a few days later took his bike and gear to his home, where I shared details of the tragic event with his wife and children.

This fatal incident brought home the full impact of *carpe diem*, or seize the day. Our lives are short and precious. We need to appreciate each moment, the joys and the sorrows, and be able to hold the tension between the two. We can enjoy our many blessings, while learning from our mistakes and failures. Together they make us real, and allow us to be an instrument of God's love as we listen to the stories of others and share our own experiences. We are all gifted in different ways, while at the same time we all struggle with our limitations. The novelist Robert Louis Stevenson wrote, "Life is not a matter of holding good cards, but of playing a poor hand well." Renowned violinist Itzhak Perlman offers this aphorism: "The challenge is how much music you can create with what you have left."

I accept who I am with all of my imperfections. I am grateful to be the person God made me, and I relish my life, family, and friends. At the same time I want to encounter new experiences and go deeper spiritually. Part of living in the *now* is being open to new possibilities for the *future*. My fitness center has a slogan: "Start where you are." The motto encourages us to come with our flabby bodies and poor aerobic conditioning, and work to improve our physical health. The same is true with our spiritual health—start the journey wherever you are and build from there. God will encourage and guide you along the way.

CHAPTER 13

Social and Economic Injustice

PAUL WRITES OF THE importance of faith, rather than religious dogma. "We see that people are acceptable to God because they have faith, and not because they obey the law" (Romans 3:28). Faith puts us in a right relationship with God and connects us with God's indwelling spirit. But as important as faith is in changing our lives and redeeming the world, Paul goes on to say that faith by itself is insufficient if it is not accompanied by compassionate action. "The only thing that counts is faith expressing itself through love" (Galatians 5:6). James, the brother of Jesus, writes in his epistle, "What good is it, my brothers, if a man claims to have faith but has no deeds . . . faith by itself, if it is not accompanied by action, is dead" (James 2:14, 17).

Many religious institutions have become stale and irrelevant because they do not reflect concern for the social needs of the day, such as income inequality, homelessness, hunger, healthcare disparity, and unequal justice for all. If these were concerns of Jesus, should they not also be concerns of Christians today? God's intention is for *all* people to flourish, not just those at the top of the social and economic pyramid.

The United States has seen wealth become concentrated in the hands of progressively fewer people. Since the 1970s, the richest Americans have grown significantly richer, while working families barely get by on flat wages. "Today, the top 1 percent of households own more wealth than the bottom 90 percent combined. That gap, between the ultrawealthy and everyone else, has only become wider in the past several decades."[1] In the U.S., 14 percent of residents and 21 percent of children live in poverty. Our society has become increasingly fractured between the haves and the have-nots, the rich and the poor, the powerful and the powerless.

For generations, as productivity increased so did real wages. Les Leopold writes, "Since the late 1970s, the average real wage for most of us has stalled. Productivity is still rising at a healthy pace, but we workers aren't getting our share of the value of what we produce. Corporate elites are siphoning off revenues for themselves—and cutting their investment in facilities, equipment, research, and workers. Had we continued to get our fair share of productivity gains, the average American non-supervisory production wage would be $1,377 per week in 2017. That's almost double the current average weekly wage of $746 (measured after inflation in 2017 dollars)."[2]

Here in the wealthiest country in the world, why are we so strapped to pay for first-rate education, child care for working parents, sick leave, health care for all, and infrastructure projects like mass transit and bridge maintenance? One major reason is that the wealthiest Americans and many corporations are not paying their fair share of taxes. The corporate share of federal taxes has dropped from 32 percent in 1952 to only 9 percent in 2016. According to a report by the D.C.-based think tank Institute on Taxation and Economic Policy (ITEP), sixty of America's biggest corporations paid no taxes in 2018, including Amazon, FedEx, IBM, Gannett, Netflix, and Delta Air Lines.[3]

"One subversive way that corporations and the wealthy have reduced their share of the tax burden is to move money offshore . . . Large corporations simply keep their global profits in subsidiaries. This can be as easy as switching accounts in Wall Street banks."[4]

1. Ingraham, "Not Only Are Americans Becoming Less Happy."

2. Leopold, *Runaway Inequality*, 24.

3. Institute on Taxation and Economic Policy , *Corporate Tax Avoidance Remains Rampant*.

4. Leopold, *Runaway Inequality*, 98.

Like corporations, rich people are adept at hiding money in offshore accounts, where it is invested virtually tax free and out of reach of the IRS. "The U.S. Public Interest Research Group (PIRG) reports we're losing about $184 billion a year to corporate and individual offshore tax evasion. That's enough money to cover tuition for students at every public university, college and community college in the country."[5]

In 1970 the top federal tax rate for individuals was 70 percent; today it is about half that rate at 37 percent. But this tells only part of the story since tax loopholes, such as "carried interest," have burgeoned in recent decades, saving billions of dollars in taxes for hedge fund managers and others in the highest echelons of business and finance. Billionaire Warren Buffett bluntly states that he pays a lower federal tax rate than his secretary. Today's wealth inequality could be addressed by closing most tax loopholes and instituting a more progressive income tax so that the rich and corporations pay a fairer share of the tax burden. Philanthropist and Microsoft co-founder Bill Gates recommends boosting the capital gains tax rate, increasing the estate tax, and initiating some form of wealth tax.

In 2011 hundreds of protesters set up camp in Zuccotti Park in New York City to highlight wealth disparity between the 1 percent and 99 percent. The Occupy Movement was an upwelling of frustration, a rallying call for the 99 percent of Americans who have little power and influence. It spawned similar protests in hundreds of cities in eighty-two countries. In the spring of 2018 the "Poor People's Campaign: A National Call for Moral Revival" occupied the Washington Mall to protest systemic poverty, racism, the war economy, and ecological devastation.

The economic inequality in the U.S. has been called America's Second Gilded Age. Clearly the disparity is a moral issue. Increasing poverty has spawned hunger, homelessness, drug abuse, and suicide, all of which have been on the rise. There has been no increase in HUD funding since 1997, despite unprecedented home mortgage defaults during the 2008 great recession and the current nationwide homeless crisis. In recent years Congress has moved to

5. Leopold, *Runaway Inequality*, 100–101.

reduce funding for food (SNAP, WIC, and school meals). By the end of 2019 fourteen states still were not participating in federal health care subsidies for their poorest residents through the Affordable Care Act. Such policy decisions are contrary to the biblical imperative to defend the poor and needy:

> I know that the Lord secures justice for the poor,
> and upholds the cause of the needy. (Psalm 140:12)

Author Stephen Mattson writes, "Godly justice is fueled by love, a love for the poor, the widow, those who are cast aside and powerless—the immigrants, refugees, homeless, sick, abandoned, and persecuted. When 'Christianity' doesn't pursue justice, it becomes complicit to evil. It protects abusers, votes for bigots, covers up wrongdoing, feeds upon corruption, preys upon the vulnerable, and seeks power rather than accountability—it looks nothing like Jesus."[6]

Whatever our political leanings, we need to approach these issues through the eyes of Jesus. A number of years ago bumper stickers appeared saying "What Would Jesus Do?" It is a good frame of reference as we wade into the turbulent waters of income disparity and concern for the needy. Federal, state, and local budgets are moral documents, indicating how we as a society choose to allocate our tax dollars. Jesus clearly had a bias for those at the bottom of the economic pyramid. He railed against the arrogance and hypocrisy of the power elite of the day, and he spoke on behalf of those who were poor, oppressed, exploited, and treated unjustly.

We are at a time in history when people of faith need to come together to stand up to the corrupting influence of money and the power it can buy in government, as well as in some corporations, nonprofit organizations, and even the church. For example, the Catholic Church in America is influenced by well-healed advocacy groups like the Napa Institute, Legatus, and the Acton Institute. *If Jesus' life and ministry are to teach us anything, it is to renounce money, power, and control.*

Martin Luther King Jr. wrote from the Birmingham jail, "Wherever the early Christians entered a town the power structure

---

6. Mattson, "Pursuing Justice as an Act of Worship."

got disturbed and immediately sought to convict them for being 'disturbers of the peace' and 'outside agitators' . . . Things are different now. The contemporary church is often a weak, ineffectual voice with an uncertain sound. So often it is the arch-defender of the status quo. Far from being disturbed by the presence of the church, the power structure of the average community is consoled by the church's silent—and often even vocal—sanction of things as they are."[7]

Will we push our churches (and synagogues and mosques) to get more engaged in the social justice issues of the day, or are we content with uplifting music and a comforting message that all is well with the world? If the church wants to be relevant, it needs to respond to the social and economic needs that everywhere engulf our society. Desmond Tutu said it best: "To be neutral in a situation of injustice is to have chosen sides already. It is to support the status quo." The world is skewed toward injustice, but God's justice will ultimately prevail. Martin Luther King Jr. stated, "The arc of the moral universe is long, but it bends toward justice."

Charity for the poor is admirable, but it is not social justice. A donation to charity is putting a Band-Aid on significant societal issues. It is handing out a fish, but not providing the opportunity for people to learn how to fish. If we see people floating in the river, our job is not simply pull them out; we need to go upstream to discover why they are falling in the river. If we see homeless folks camped in our parks and byways, what does it say about wage disparity, a shortage of affordable housing, the failure of our mental health system, a dearth of drug rehabilitation programs for addicts, the need for job retraining programs, and the number of veterans not getting necessary services?

Going upstream involves taking a hard look at structural biases that are built into our system and that discriminate against the poor, people of color, those who are illiterate, the mentally ill, those who speak a foreign language, the handicapped, and those with differing sexual orientation. Jesus defended those who have been

---

7. King, "Letter from Birmingham Jail," in *I Have a Dream*, 97.

victims of discrimination. We have to ask ourselves, what is our role to help these folks find a place at the table?

Some social services that are offered to impoverished people can be provided by local churches, or other religious institutions, or charitable nonprofit organizations. But many basic needs such as housing, healthcare, food supplement programs, education, and early childhood intervention are too complex and too expensive to be left to local charities. It falls to national, state, and local governments to fill the void in meeting the needs of those who are unable to provide for themselves. The public sector is further needed to set policy on social justice issues like immigration, human rights, and exposure to toxic chemicals. Some issues are global in scope, needing international cooperation, such as climate disruption, which is affecting all inhabitants of our planet, but especially those who are already living on the margins.

Author Charles Gutenson puts it this way: "Any genuinely Christian position on the role of public institutions and policies will have to reckon with the fact that so many (too many, both globally and nationally) are in poverty, that proper health care is increasingly difficult to obtain, and that we too eagerly and too often find reasons to go to war. Additionally, we will have to articulate a consistent agenda that affirms the sanctity of life, finds ways to encourage and empower families to flourish, and develops strategies for tending to the good creation with which God has entrusted us."[8]

Here in my home state of Oregon, we have formed a nonpartisan education and advocacy group called Oregon Coalition of Christian Voices to monitor the Oregon Legislature to ensure that its policies benefit the common good rather than special interests. We try to look at proposed bills from the viewpoint of poor people whose voice is often not heard. We help marginalized people testify when their lives will be directly impacted by proposed legislation. Our vision is of Oregon transformed by a network of Christian organizations, boldly proclaiming the fullness of Christ's vision for

8. Gutenson, *Christians and the Common Good*, 16–17.

humanity, and working together with other faiths to shape public policy for the common good.[9]

Faith is deeply personal, but as Jesus made abundantly clear, it is about social justice as much as personal salvation. Sojourners founder Jim Wallis is fond of saying, "Faith is always personal but never private." People of faith are called to express their faith by engaging in public policy and speaking up for "the least of these," our brothers and sisters. Morality crosses the line between the separation of church and state, and is essential to both.

When politics gets messy and divisive, it's time to circle back to Jesus. He spent his life among common people and outcasts and railed against the arrogance and hypocrisy of religious leaders, the power elite of the day. His activism and outspokenness inevitably clashed with the authorities, and he paid the price with his life. He demonstrated ultimate humility as he submitted to beatings and mocking and hung naked and bleeding on the cross. His sacrifice is a powerful testament to living by faith and dying for humanity.

The prophets, too, were outspoken about social justice. "And what does the Lord require of you? To act justly and to love mercy and to walk humbly with your God" (Micah 6: 8). "But let justice roll on like a river, righteousness like a never-failing stream" (Amos 5:24). Scripture is clear that we are called to love both God and neighbor. Our neighbor includes those who are vulnerable, like children, the elderly, the sick, and those in prison. Our neighbors may be outsiders, immigrants and refugees, those who don't speak our language, or who have a different faith. People of faith can hardly ignore the plight of children taken from their parents and put in detention camps at the U.S.-Mexico border.

Jesus said, "Whatever you do for one of the least of these brothers (and sisters) of mine, you do for me" (Matthew 25:40). I don't think Jesus is talking about simply making a contribution to charity, as worthy as that may be. I think he means we are to get to know the poor and homeless and those with different racial and ethnic identities. We are to care for them like a neighbor, loving

---

9. For more information, go to www.occv.org.

them and sharing our relative abundance. It is one thing to give to the poor; it is another to befriend and get to know them.

Charles Gutenson writes, "The story of the rich man and Lazarus in Luke 16 makes it clear that God's expectations for those who have much is that they will use their wealth to benefit others . . . The difficulties the rich man finds himself in by the end of the story do not arise because he did something evil to Lazarus. Rather, they arise simply because he had the resources to help and did not."[10] We who have been born into relative privilege have an obligation to speak up for people of color who face discrimination in housing, loans, criminal justice, and job applications, and for immigrants who may not be paid their full wages, afraid to report the abuse because they or a family member may be undocumented.

In his final Memphis speech, Martin Luther King Jr. talked about the Good Samaritan and asked, "The question is not, 'If I stop to help this man in need, what will happen to me?' The question is 'If I do not stop to help the sanitation workers, what will happen to them.'" To love our neighbors is to put their needs before our own. For people of faith our intent should be to live a life of caring and service, which means leading more with our heart than with our head. Sometimes we may fail in our efforts to serve the poor and vulnerable; justice often is not easy or successful. But as Mahatma Gandhi taught, "Joy lies in the fight, in the attempt, in the suffering involved, not in the victory itself."

10. Gutenson, *Christians and the Common Good*, 76.

CHAPTER 14

Racial Injustice

IN AUGUST 1619, JUST twelve years after the English settled James-town, Virginia, the Jamestown colonists bought twenty to thirty enslaved Africans from what is now the country of Angola. This was the first of four hundred thousand enslaved Africans who would be sold in America. Slave labor drove the remarkable prosperity of the colonies, not only in the South that grew 66 percent of the world's cotton supply, but also in the Northern textile mills where cotton was processed. Our great nation was built on the backs of slaves, who also built railroads, plantations, state houses, the U.S. Capitol Building, and prestigious universities like Georgetown.

Slavery has been called "America's original sin," although in fact the country was built on the dual sins of slavery and the deci-mation of indigenous peoples by force and by disease with expro-priation of their lands. Founding fathers like George Washington, Thomas Jefferson, and James Madison were slave owners them-selves. It must have been awkward for Jefferson to pen these words for the Declaration of Independence: "We hold these truths to be self-evident, that all men are created equal, that they are endowed by their Creator with certain unalienable Rights, that among these are Life, Liberty and pursuit of Happiness."

How did the white men who drafted the Declaration of In-dependence justify the incongruity of their call for equality with the reality of chattel slavery, where slaves had no rights, no claim to their own children, could be bought and sold at will, and could be tortured, raped, and murdered without any legal protections or consequences? The country's founders fabricated a justification that Black people were subhuman, the products of a slave race. The framers of the U.S. Constitution never mentioned slavery but wrote in article 1, section 2, paragraph 3 that people of African descent are worth "three fifths of all other Persons." Our country was founded on the principle of dehumanizing blacks—no wonder it is so deeply ingrained in our psyche even today.

The view that Black people were an inferior race was reinforced by the Supreme Court in 1857 in *Dred Scott v. Sandford*, which ruled that black people, whether enslaved or free, came from a slave race. The court "ruled that no person of African descent could ever become a citizen of the United States, on the grounds that the framers of the Constitution had viewed Africans as 'being of an inferior order, and altogether unfit to associate with the white race, either in social or political relations; and so far inferior, that they had no rights which the white man was bound to respect.'"[1]

Nikole Hannah-Jones in an essay for the August 14, 2019 edition of *New York Times Magazine*, writes, "This belief, that black people were not merely enslaved but were a slave race, became the root of the endemic racism that we still cannot purge from this nation to this day. If black people could not ever be citizens, if they were a caste apart from all other humans, then they did not require the rights bestowed by the constitution." Clearly, white supremacy has deep structural roots in the institutions and attitudes of our country.

Bryan Stevenson is quoted in Daniel Hill's book *White Awake* as saying, "The whole narrative of white supremacy was created during the era of slavery. It was a necessary theory to make white Christian people feel comfortable with their ownership of other human beings. And we created a narrative of racial difference in this country to sustain slavery, and even people who didn't own slaves bought into that narrative, including people in the North."[2]

---

1. Lepore, *This America*, 58–59.
2. Hill, *White Awake*, 56.

Following the Emancipation Proclamation, defeat of the Confederacy, and Reconstruction, Jim Crow laws were enacted across the South to assure racial segregation and to restrict the voting rights of African-Americans, policies upheld by the Supreme Court in *Plessy v. Ferguson* in 1896. Despite little or no provocation, widespread lynching of blacks was conducted with impunity to terrorize black people into submission.

Jill Lepore writes that the Klu Klux Klan, originally formed in the 1860s, was inspired by the pro Confederacy film *The Birth of a Nation* in 1915 and was reborn "under the banner of 'true Americanism.' Its object was 'to unite white male persons, native-born Gentile citizens of the United States . . . to maintain forever white supremacy' and 'conserve, protect and maintain the distinctive institutions, rights, privileges, principles, traditions and ideals of pure Americanism.'"[3]

You may ask, why are we spending so much time focused on American history? But to understand the rise of white supremacy today, we have to understand that the narrative of racial difference is deeply embedded in our historical roots. Daniel Hill traces this narrative as a thread through American history. "During slave days, the narrative poisoned our minds to justify owning other human beings. In the late 1800s, it poisoned our minds to participate in lynchings and to watch as people of color (mostly black) were executed publicly without a legal trial . . . It poisoned our minds to enact Jim Crow laws and to watch as whites-only spaces were built and preserved throughout society. In the later 1900s, it poisoned our minds to criminalize young men of color and establish America as the country with the highest incarceration rate on the planet. In the present, the narrative has produced endless tragedies, including the deaths of Michael Brown, Rekia Boyd, Eric Garner, Sandra Bland, Tamir Rice, and many more."[4]

The series of police shootings of African-Americans by white officers led to the Black Lives Matter movement, which highlights differential police use of force against Blacks. So here's the rub:

3. Lapore, *This America*, 86.
4. Hill, *White Awake*, 58.

Genesis says that God created us all in God's image. No exceptions—all are children of one God. Race is a human construct, designed to justify slavery and to promote the concept of superiority and inferiority. Racism is rooted in fear of losing one's privileged position in society, of giving up power and control, of losing a means to amass wealth. Racism could not be further from God's abundant love for all creation and for God's plan to bring unity and wholeness to the world. When we assign differing value to human beings, our attitudes and actions are contrary to the will of God.

In the decade following World War II, the U.S. economy boomed and three million veterans received free higher education through the GI Bill. Erin Blakemore notes, "While the GI Bill's language did not specifically exclude African-American veterans from its benefits, it was structured in a way that ultimately shut doors for the 1.2 million black veterans who had bravely served their country during World War II, in segregated ranks . . . Though the bill helped white Americans prosper and accumulate wealth in the postwar years, it didn't deliver on that promise for veterans of color. In fact, the wide disparity in the bill's implementation ended up helping drive growing gaps in wealth, education and civil rights between white and black Americans."[5] Veterans returning from WWII also bought houses financed by the Federal Housing Administration (FHA), but less than 2 percent of FHA loans were made available to non-white home buyers. Much of the postwar housing boom, like Levittown, was off limits to blacks. Realtors and bankers knew the unwritten codes to whom they could show houses and loan money for mortgages. Black neighborhoods were "redlined," meaning they were ineligible for mortgages. America was racially segregated, and remains so in much of the country today. The housing bubble that led up to the housing bust of 2008 exploited the financial vulnerability of blacks and other minorities. Bankers devised new housing investments based on high-interest rate, subprime mortgages that especially targeted black and Latino would-be buyers. These loans became all the rage as mortgage brokers and banks focused on duping these would-be buyers, capitalizing on their fears that

5. Blakemore, "How the GI Bill's Promise Was Denied."

they would have trouble finding conventional mortgages. Here's how a *New York Times* editorial explained it: "Pricing discrimination—illegally charging minority customers more for loans and other services than similarly qualified whites are charged—is a longstanding problem. It grew to outrageous proportions during the bubble years. Studies by consumer advocates found that large numbers of minority borrowers who were eligible for affordable, traditional loans were routinely steered toward ruinously priced subprime loans that they would never be able to repay."[6]

For those of us who were born into white privilege, we have made assumptions of equality in "the land of the free," where we have been taught that anyone can succeed based on motivation and ability. As a white male living in a predominately white state and relatively isolated from discrimination against minorities, I was shocked in the 1980s when a black friend told me that he had been denied entrance into a local night club, and that his teenage son was routinely stopped by police because of racial profiling. Today I am no longer shocked, but rather struggle with and lament the slow progress we have made toward racial equality and justice.

Stephen Mattson writes, "Privilege insulates white Christians from the immense impact that racism has on others. Conversely, no matter how people of color think, feel, or act, their reality is determined by a factor well beyond their control—their race or ethnicity. This radical contrast based simply on the color of one's skin is just one example of white privilege. In some cases, the term *white privilege* itself is inappropriate—not because it's too controversial but because it's too tame and too sanitary and too individualistic. A more appropriate term may be *white supremacy,* which conveys the systemically racist nature of social structures."[7]

We prefer to stigmatize the ideology of white supremacy as residing in hate-filled, ignorant racists. Most of us white people are willing to admit that we have been beneficiaries of white privilege, but we bristle at the notion that we may be tainted by white supremacy. We get defensive if someone suggests that we may be

6. "Fair Lending and Accountability," *New York Times* editoral, quoted in Leopold, *Runaway Inequality,* 144–45.

7. Mattson, *Great Reckoning,* 47.

inadvertently, or overtly, complicit. Daniel Hill writes, "The only way we can move past defensiveness about white supremacy is to realize what it is and what it is not . . . When we hear about white supremacy, superiority, and anything else in that lexical family, our natural reaction is to assume we're being attacked. But once we can identify it as a system, principality, and power of darkness, we realize there's nothing left to defend. In fact, we realize that our own interests are at stake, for that system dehumanizes us as much as it does anyone else."[8]

The racist ideology of white superiority/supremacy is currently festering like an open wound in America and elsewhere. While simmering prejudice and outright violence has often been directed at African-Americans, other groups of color, including Native Americans, Mexicans, Chinese, Japanese, and other groups, have also felt the sting of white supremacy and xenophobia during our country's history.

Distrust and hatred of those who are different is further compounded by the epidemic of mass shootings perpetrated by resentful white male loners who target minorities, such as black worshippers at a predominately African-American Charleston church (2015), gays at an Orlando nightclub (2016), Jews worshiping at a Pittsburg synagogue (2018), and Muslims at prayer in Christchurch, New Zealand (2019). Loners and losers have also randomly targeted young school children at Sandy Hook Elementary School in Newtown, Connecticut (2012), concertgoers in Las Vegas (2017), and teenagers at Marjory Stoneman Douglas High School in Parkland, Florida (2018), just to name a few of the mass shootings in recent years. The Internet has provided a platform for disaffected, angry white males to voice their resentment and advocate for extreme, nihilistic actions. The ready availability of military-style assault weapons with large-capacity ammunition magazines has made the mayhem all the more deadly.

It's too early to predict the outcome of the epic struggle between good and evil that is playing out in our world today. When we read shocking headlines of mass violence, we often overlook the

8. Hill, *White Awake*, 148.

majority of humans who thrive on social interaction with family, friends, and neighbors and who work on issues of civil rights, racial justice, and peace. Despite all of our failings, we humans seem to be wired to want to do good and to be of service to others. The hand of God is at work through acts of sacrificial love and kindness.

When we introduce God into the equation, the odds of this battle tilt in favor of righteousness and peace. Through faith we believe that God will ultimately prevail over the powers and principalities of darkness. As collective children of God, we believe there is more that unites us than divides us. Jesus taught that love has the redemptive power to overcome fear and hate. Martin Luther King Jr. preached, "Darkness cannot drive out darkness, only light can do that. Hate cannot drive out hate, only love can do that."

We see the progress that has been made on world hunger, poverty, and education, especially for girls and women in low-income countries. We have witnessed remarkable world health advances through cooperative ventures by public and private partnerships, including vaccines that have eradicated smallpox, have curtailed many common childhood infectious diseases, and have reduced polio to a few dozen cases per year. Villages around the world are receiving clean water, sanitation, and electricity for the first time through a variety of programs. There is ample reason to hope and believe in a future where reconciliation and justice will prevail.

The prophet Zechariah may be the first to use the phrase "prisoners of hope" (Zechariah 9:12). "In an interview with *Frontline*, Harvard professor Dr. Cornel West, another modern-day freedom fighter, was asked if he was optimistic about where America is heading. Here is what he answered, 'I am not optimistic, but I've never been optimistic about humankind or America. The evidence never looks good in terms of forces for good actually becoming prominent. But I am a prisoner of hope, and that's very different. I believe that we do have signs of hope, and that the evidence is underdetermined. We have to make a leap of faith beyond the evidence and try to energize one another so we can accent the best in one another. But that is what being a prisoner of hope is all about.'"[9]

9. Hill, *White Awake*, 158–59.

CHAPTER 15

Violence and Nonviolence

WE LIVE IN A culture of violence. Violence is glamorized on TV, movies, and video games, where killing is often portrayed as sport and entertainment. The number of mass shootings in the U.S. continues to escalate and far exceeds any other industrialized country. Americans collectively own over three million high-powered, semiautomatic assault rifles, adapted from military weapons and designed to kill and maim people with frightening efficiency. Social media and the Internet are used to violate others through bullying, vicious lies, fake news, and attacks to undermine the democratic process. America's most popular sport is football, known to cause chronic traumatic brain syndrome and other serious injuries.

Sixty-one percent of the 2019 U.S federal discretionary federal budget goes to military spending, compared to 5 percent for education, 5 percent for health, 7 percent for veterans' benefits, 2 percent for science, and 2 percent for diplomacy and foreign aid. Nine countries (U.S., Russia, the U.K., France, China, India, Pakistan, Israel, and North Korea) collectively have a stockpile of 14,500 nuclear weapons, of which 4,120 are deployed and ready to launch within 15 minutes, commonly known as being on "hair-trigger alert." The U.S. is planning to spend $1.2 trillion rebuilding its entire nuclear weapons arsenal.

This brief reality check on violence and militarism doesn't sound much like the Lord's Prayer where we say, "Thy kingdom come on earth as it is in heaven." Quite the contrary, it is easy to feel overwhelmed, powerless, and apathetic. I suspect the Israelites felt much the same way living under the Roman occupation in Palestine. I have wondered if God chose that particular moment in history to send Jesus to dispel a sense of powerlessness and bring hope to the downtrodden.

Once we recognize that violence has engulfed our society at so many levels, we can personally choose an alternative path of nonviolence. Martin Luther King Jr. warned that "our choice is between non-violence and non-existence." King called the principle of nonviolent resistance the "guiding light of our movement. Christ furnished the spirit and motivation while Gandhi furnished the method." Preacher and civil rights activist John M. Perkins says, "We cannot have homeland security until we recognize that the whole world is our homeland."

To advocate for nonviolence we can come together in solidarity with vulnerable populations to speak out against injustice, racism, and bigotry. Some people may choose to participate in nonviolent vigils or marches to visibly express their principles and beliefs. Others may advocate for nonviolent civil action, as clearly stated and demonstrated by Mohandas Gandhi and Martin Luther King Jr., which can be a powerful and effective force for change. It commits to peaceful protest that honors and respects the inherent worth and dignity of every human being. Images of nonviolent protesters being attacked by police dogs, billy clubs, and water cannon in Selma, Alabama in March 1965 grabbed the nation's attention, and led to passage of the landmark Voting Rights Act of 1965. Other methods of expressing our beliefs include speaking out on social media, contacting elected representatives at every level of government, engaging the press by writing letters to the editor of one's local newspaper, raising issues at town hall meetings, joining and working with peace and justice organizations, and opposing offensive and derogatory language and actions whenever we see and hear them. For more information on nonviolent resistance, I recommend George Lakey's clear and effective primer on organizing strategies, *How We Win* (2018).

American culture has glorified guns as mythical symbols of rugged individualism, harkening back to the days of the Wild West. Americans privately own about three hundred million firearms, nearly enough for every man, woman, and child, whatever their age, training, or mental health status. Firearm deaths and injuries are a public health crisis in the U.S. with 39,740 gun deaths in 2018, the most recent year for which statistics are available. Congress has done a disservice to the American people by restricting the CDC (Center for Disease Control and Prevention) from tracking firearm injuries and deaths since passage of the Dickey Amendment in 1996, effectively cutting federal funding for research to study gun violence. Why are background checks not routinely required for gun purchases, including at gun shows and online sales, to screen out felons and those with serious mental illness? How is it that Americans possess a few million AK-47 and AR-15 military assault weapons, whose lethal force makes no sense outside the military? If these high-powered weapons were ever used for hunting, there would be nothing left of the carcass. And why do we allow firearm magazines that hold more than ten rounds, causing more lives to be lost in schools, concerts, and places of worship with frightening efficiency?

Since the male brain is not fully developed until the mid-twenties, why do we allow the sale of firearms to minors? Public health ads could do much to promote the safe storage of firearms to keep them out of the hands of children, criminals, and those who are suicidal. Trigger locks can prevent a firearm from being discharged by anyone except the owner—why are they not routinely used? In my experience, some of the strongest proponents of sensible gun safety measures are responsible hunters and sportsmen. Our country has taken many public health measures to reduce motor vehicle deaths, like seat belts and children's car seats; so much could be done to reduce firearm injuries and deaths without trampling on Second Amendment rights of gun ownership.

Capital punishment is another form of violence that is deeply ingrained in our culture. It promotes the idea that violence is an appropriate solution to social problems, although the death penalty is used disproportionately against minorities and poor people. The unending appeals process for inmates on death row is far more expensive than the cost of housing inmates with life sentences. The resources saved could be better spent to improve the criminal justice system. Most Christians and many people of other faith traditions oppose the death penalty, believing that all human life is sacred and created by God, and that reconciliation and redemption are potential pathways for all individuals.[1]

Many injustices have been committed over the years with the sentencing and execution of innocent people. Since 1973 DNA testing has aided in the exoneration of at least 166 innocent people on death row, but we don't know how many other innocents have been executed. The reality is that our human judicial system is flawed and can make fatal mistakes. Capital punishment has been shown to be arbitrary and racially biased, and it fails to give closure to victim's families. Institutional violence, rooted in the death penalty, is not the way of reconciliation and the cross.

Views on the death penalty are not defined by a conservative/progressive, Republican/Democrat split. Jared Olsen wrote in a New York Times op-ed article, "A long-held stereotype is that conservatives favor capital punishment, while liberals oppose it. But that doesn't accord with reality: In recent years, more conservatives have come to realize that capital punishment conflicts irreconcilably with their principles of valuing life, fiscal responsibility and limited government. Many conservatives also recognize that the death penalty inflicts extreme and unnecessary trauma on the

---

1. Many Christian denominations have taken an official position in opposition to the death penalty, including American Baptist Church (but not Southern Baptist Convention), Roman Catholic Church, Christian Church (Disciples of Christ), Church of the Brethren, Episcopal Church, Evangelical Lutheran Church in America (but not the Lutheran Church: Missouri Synod), Mennonite Church, United Methodist Church, Presbyterian Church (USA), Religious Society of Friends (Quakers), and United Church of Christ. Most traditionally black churches oppose the death penalty, including A.M.E. Church, A.M.E. Zion Church, C.M.E. Church, and Church of God of Prophecy. Virtually all Jewish traditions have rejected capital punishment, including Conservative, Reform, and Reconstructionist movements in the United States. In 2001, Orthodox Jewish leaders called for a moratorium on any further executions. The Unitarian Universalist Association opposes the death penalty. Most Buddhists find capital punishment incompatible with their ethical principles.

family members of victims and the correctional employees who have the job of taking the prisoner's life."[2]

Jesus is clear where he stands on killing and violence. Stephen Mattson notes, "Killing goes against Christ's very nature of bringing life. When you carry a sidearm, or support warfare, or vote for the death penalty, you are declaring that you are okay with killing a creation of God—okay with destroying someone whom God knows and loves. So how did Christians—especially certain groups of them—gain a reputation for being pro-war, pro-gun, pro-capital punishment, and pro-death?"[3]

A discussion of violence today must also include abuse of others by sexual violence. Some of the most notorious examples reported by the media include children abused by priests, women assaulted by film producer Harvey Weinstein (the #metoo movement), and underage girls and young women abused by financier and convicted sex offender Jeffery Epstein. But lets be clear that anyone who is in a position of power and authority over another may be tempted to abuse their position for sexual gratification. Whenever people use their money, power, and influence to manipulate others who are vulnerable and weaker, it is a sin in the eyes of God. The heart of God resides within each person's soul, and to degrade and abuse another is to violate God's indwelling spirit.

While the scope of this book cannot include all forms of violence, we can hardly ignore violence against the natural world, including the pollution of our planet and climate disruption. Genesis 2:15 declares, "The Lord God took the man and put him in the Garden of Eden to work it and take care of it." God's intention is for humans to be stewards of God's magnificent creation, but sadly, we have done a poor job of stewardship. Our rivers, skies, and land are polluted with toxic chemicals, and our seas are awash with huge islands of floating plastic. Many pesticides are toxic to children, and some are killing off bees and other pollinators with dire consequences to plant life and the food chain on which we and other living creatures depend. We are recklessly cutting down

2. Olsen, "We Should End Federal Executions."

3. Mattson, *Great Reckoning*, 120.

tropical forests, the lungs of the planet where carbon dioxide (CO_2) is converted to oxygen, for the misguided purposes of grazing cattle, growing soybeans, and establishing palm oil plantations. We expose our children to lead in water pipes, diesel emissions from trucks, school buses and other engines, and hundreds of industrial pollutants, including heavy metals that can cause learning disabilities, lowered IQ, hyperactivity, and attention deficit.

Approximately eighty thousand chemicals have been developed over the past eighty years—some that are carcinogenic, cause birth defects, suppress the immune system, or decrease fertility—but only several hundred have had been adequately tested for toxicity by the Environmental Protection Agency (EPA). Many cancers are hormone sensitive, and are exacerbated by hormone-mimicking chemicals, known as hormone disrupters. The problem now is that we live in such a toxic soup of chemicals that it is difficult to prove cause and effect between any one chemical and a given cancer. Many European countries have adopted the precautionary principle, where new chemicals must be tested for potential toxicity before they are released for production. Unfortunately, the U.S. permits the manufacture and use of untested chemicals in consumer products, only to later discover their toxicity and harm to human health. Examples include BPA (bisphenol A) in water bottles, Teflon in cooking pans, and flame retardants in children's pajamas, furniture foam, and electronic products. Why should we allow the chemical industry to use children and adults as guinea pigs to evaluate the toxicity of new chemical products?

The run-off of fertilizers into rivers, lakes, and seas has caused massive algae blooms of phytoplankton and algae that deplete the water of oxygen. These hypoxic dead zones contain so little dissolved oxygen that fish, shellfish, and other aquatic life cannot survive. Some of the areas most affected in the U.S. are the Gulf of Mexico, Chesapeake Bay, Lake Erie, and off the coast of Oregon.

One of the gravest threats facing our planet today is climate disruption. This is not a benign warming trend, but is a moral issue with epic consequences for life on Earth. The extraction and burning of fossil fuels (coal, oil, gas, wood) is heating the planet by the release of carbon dioxide, methane, and other greenhouse gases into the atmosphere where the gases trap heat rather than allowing it to radiate into space. Consequently, glaciers are melting and sea levels are rising, threatening costal cities like Venice and Miami and inundating island nations. As carbon dioxide is adsorbed by the oceans, the water becomes more acidic, killing off coral reefs, which are the habitat for much marine plant and animal life. Warming oceans add energy to tropical storms, causing more intense and destructive hurricanes with flooding and dislocation of affected populations.

Warmer climates also breed disease-bearing insects, which move into ever-expanding areas, exposing new populations to diseases like malaria, dengue, West Nile virus, and Eastern equine encephalitis. The warming and drying of the planet are causing wildfires, from California to Australia, which are becoming more common, more intense, and harder to contain. Such fires release large quantities of CO_2 into the atmosphere, further contributing to climate disruption, and exacerbating asthma and emphysema in humans. As forests are cut and glaciers recede, water resources are drying up in many parts of the world, leading to more frequent droughts. Some lands that were formerly cultivated are now too dry to support agriculture, increasing the risk of famine. In three visits to a remote hospital in Sierra Leone, West Africa over the span of forty-five years, I have witnessed the transformation of some areas from lush jungles teeming with monkeys to an arid landscape barren of trees and most other vegetation.

With climate disruption, comes heightened tension over food supplies and water rights to rivers, lakes, and aquifers. Populations are forced to move to survive, causing conflict over the resettlement of refugees, many of whom end up in city slums or refugee camps that often lack sanitation, fresh drinking water, and adequate food. This dislocation of people is leading to an unprecedented humanitarian crisis, threatening national security and economic stability. Tensions between countries have been rising over immigration and refugee resettlement.

Climate disruption clearly is a social justice issue: the people most affected are those who already live in hot, tropical climates or on the margins of society. The poor, sick, and elderly are particularly vulnerable, as they tend to live in poorly ventilated buildings devoid of fans or air conditioning. In the storm surge of Hurricane Katrina in 2005, over one million people were displaced and more than eighteen hundred died. The people who suffered the most were poor people, living in the Lower Ninth Ward of New Orleans, which housed the largest percentage of African-Americans.

If humans are to be stewards of God's creation, how is it that we can allow climate disruption, the extinction of species, and the pollution of our planet? For people of faith who believe in a just and merciful God, this should be a moral and spiritual dilemma of utmost concern. Our destructive practices are leading to changes that may well become irreversible. Charles Gutenson writes, "We may not simply exploit the earth for our own gain; rather we are to tend to it, care for it, and remember that future generations will benefit or suffer based upon how well we exercise that stewardship."[4] A consensus of the world's scientists say that the consequences of climate disruption are "virtually inevitable" unless we make a dramatic shift to renewable energy. At a time of global crisis, why is organized religion not forcefully speaking out about the abuses that are ravaging our planet? A few churches and synagogues are actively engaged, but too many can't get beyond token recycling projects that have a negligible impact on the scope of the problem. Surely God must weep over the destruction of God's creation. Some politicians have chosen to politicize climate like it were an abstract issue, when in fact preventing the destruction of our planet should be among our highest priorities.

Theologian Ched Myers takes a biblical perspective, calling for collective repentance for the sin of precipitating a global catastrophe. In a May 2018 blog Myers writes, "I prefer the adage of old St. John Chrysostome: 'Sin is followed by shame; repentance is followed by boldness.' We cannot afford to be stuck in shame responses to our sinful hardheartedness and class/race complicity; they only paralyze us. True repentance leads to bold action: to recover enough of a sense of Beloved Community with earth to intervene in our own collective and individual addictions; to stand with the poor

4. Gutenson, *Christians and the Common Good*, 61.

and people of color who are affected first and worst by the climate plagues we generate; and to resist the carbon Pharaohs—our own leaders and our own deeply entrenched compulsions."[5] Myers adds, "The ecological endgame that stalks our history puts humanity in a watershed moment that demands serious, sustained engagement from Christians; we must choose between denial and discipleship. Both our love for the Creator and the interlocking crises of global warming, peak 'everything,' and widening ecological degradation should compel us to make environmental justice and sustainability integral to *everything* we do as disciples."[6]

Politicians, pundits, and fossil fuel apologists have frittered away precious decades since scientists first sounded the alarm about climate disruption in the 1970s. There is no guarantee that the planet can be saved from overheating caused by the burning of fossil fuels. But if we choose to do nothing, we doom future generations and other living creatures to an uninhabitable planet.

In summary, God requires that we move from violence to nonviolence in relation to each other, other life forms, and the planet itself. We are all in this together—ordinary people with a vision of a just, sustainable, and peaceful world. Martin Luther King Jr. preached that we must not let our voices be drowned out by "the evils of racism, poverty, militarism, and environmental degradation." Jesus tells us we need to meet acts of hatred and violence with acts of love and reconciliation. If we observe racism, bigotry, hatred, or abuse of people, or if we are aware of violence against the planet, we should not remain passive bystanders but speak up. We must intervene on behalf of all who are in need, offering ourselves as an intermediary of God's love and concern. Jesus put it this way:

> Blessed are the merciful, for they will be shown mercy.
> Blessed are the pure in heart, for they will see God.
> Blessed are the peacemakers, for they will be called sons of God.
> Blessed are those who are persecuted because of righteousness, for theirs is the kingdom of heaven.
> (the Beatitudes, from the Sermon on the Mount, Matthew 5:7–10)

5. Myers, "Nature against Empire."
6. Myers, *Watershed Discipleship*; see https://watersheddiscipleship.org.

CHAPTER 16

The Fullness of Life

WHEN WE WERE YOUNG, we enjoyed doing cartwheels and back-flips. My eleven-year-old granddaughter doesn't walk as much as she dances wherever she goes. As we get older, our bodies get stiffer and less flexible—hardly news to most anyone reading this book! When my muscles are tight, I risk back injury if I reach into the trunk of my car for a heavy object or pick up a box of books on the floor. It is incumbent on us to stretch regularly to keep our muscles, tendons, and ligaments supple. Personally, I do about fifteen minutes of stretching every morning, which is immensely helpful, especially if supplemented with aerobic exercise (walking, running, biking, swimming, etc.) and working out with weights. These measures benefit our cardiovascular system, reduce osteoporosis, improve mental function, and control weight.

Living one's faith also requires stretching and exercise. We quickly get stiff and out of shape if faith is not built into our daily routine. Having a time of prayer and meditation is an essential part of my early morning routine, nourishing my soul and preparing me for the day's activities and encounters. An awareness of God's presence doesn't store well, like in a battery, but needs to be constantly tapped and replenished. It is an ongoing dynamic, or else it becomes depleted, static, and as stiff as our bodies.

The Bible teaches us to consider our body as a holy temple that houses the presence of God. We often hear of "mind, body and spirit" as integral factors that need to be developed to make us whole beings. We can't take our physical and mental health, nor our faith, for granted, but need to be intentional about developing and fostering these interwoven aspects of a fully integrated self. A commitment to stretching our body and deepening our faith are not additional chores to be added to our already busy lives. Instead they are fundamental, liberating, life-sustaining habits that improve our lives and allow us to function at our full capacity.

Like anything else worth doing in life, faith takes effort and persistence. If we don't demand anything of our bodies, they will take the path of least resistance and become weak and flabby, and our joints will become stiff. So too, building our faith takes commitment, including study, prayer, meditation, and sharing with others. Our faith becomes vibrant and foundational when it is tested in everyday living and is honed in service to others.

We should never get too comfortable in our faith; it is not about stability and security. Rather we must be flexible to see where the hand of God is at work and feel challenged to respond. Marrs Hill pastor Rob Bell says, "Times change. God doesn't change, but times do. We learn and grow, and the world around us shifts, and the Christian faith is alive only when it is listening, morphing, innovating, letting go of whatever has gotten in the way of Jesus and embracing whatever will help us be more and more the people God wants us to be."[1]

The tent of Christianity is broad and inclusive. Stephen Mattson notes, "Christianity is a world wide community of billions of people who speak different languages, value different cultural beliefs, practice different traditions, but all worship the same God. Christianity isn't an American religion. It isn't a white religion. It isn't an English-based religion. It isn't constrained—despite the efforts of many to do so—by any demographic factor, physical trait, political movement, social rank, financial status, race, culture, state or society."[2]

1. Bell, *Velvet Elvis*, 11.
2. Mattson, *Great Reckoning*, 109.

Whether we acknowledge it or not, most of us in America and Europe live a life of abundance. We simply don't comprehend how good we have it. Kings and emperors of ages past had nothing comparable to our central heating, modern plumbing, clean water, and access to fresh food year round. We have come to take our mobility in cars, planes, and mass transit for granted. Computers and the Internet have given us access to vast amounts of information at the touch of our fingers. Unlimited news and entertainment are available with a click of our remote.

For some of us it takes a trip to a poor African county, or to a slum in Mexico, or even a frank conversation with homeless people on the streets of an American city to realize how privileged we are. Youth returning from work projects in Guatemala or Haiti often have a whole new appreciation for the abundance of their lives, compared to the relative scarcity abroad. Back home they relish the pleasure of a hot shower, the luxury of a refrigerator, the comfort of their own bed, and the convenience of a cell phone. They appreciate the blessings that they took for granted all along.

Personally, I have an unhealthy habit of stressing out over whether I may be late for an appointment. I compensate by driving or biking faster than is prudent, sometimes losing my focus about the purpose of the meeting. It is a self-defeating habit, concentrating on a scarcity of time, rather than an abundance of opportunity. It is so contrary to what Jesus taught: "Who of you by worrying can add a single hour to his life?" (Luke 12:25). Instead, we can choose to appreciate God's providence and live in the richness and fullness of life. When we choose to live with a sense of abundance, humbly expressing gratitude along the way, we are far more likely to be on a wavelength where God can use our talents.

Humility is an essential quality that opens us up to God. Recognizing our own weakness, foolishness and sinfulness allows us to invite God into our lives. Paul wrote to the Corinthians, "Brothers, think of what you were when you were called. Not many of you were wise by human standards; not many were influential; not many were of noble birth. But God chose the foolish things of the world to shame the wise; God chose the weak things of the world to shame the strong" (1 Corinthians 1:26–27).

Arrogance shuts us down by asserting that we are quite sufficient without God's intervention. It seems that God reaches out to all people, but the arrogant often have deaf ears. It is the folks who recognize their own needs and weaknesses who are more likely to respond to God's call. Jesus said, "It is not the healthy who need a doctor, but the sick" (Matthew 9:12).

One of my favorite stories in the Bible is about the plight of the woman who had been hemorrhaging for twelve years (Luke 8:43–48). There is a crush of people all around Jesus, and the woman doesn't want to disturb him. She figures if she can just touch the edge of his cloak, she will be cured. When she does so, her bleeding immediately stops. She is ready to slip back into the crowd unnoticed, but then she is mortified when Jesus calls out, "Who touched me?" With terror in her heart, she falls at his feet and admits that she is the one who touched his garment. She did not want to be the center of attention, but now she has to face Jesus and pay the consequences of her desperate act. She confesses and awaits his mercy, a great example for the rest of us when we pray for forgiveness and healing. Jesus then speaks gently to the woman and tells her, "Daughter, your faith has healed you. Go in peace." When we humble ourselves before the Lord, amazing outcomes are possible. God can use us in wondrous ways, doing things beyond our own capabilities and experience.

I chuckle when I see the bumper sticker saying, "Expect Miracles." In the mid-1980s the city of Salem established a sister city relationship with Simferopol in the Crimea, then part of the Soviet Union. It was at the height of the Cold War, and we wanted to get to know Soviet citizens not as enemies, but as people with families, similar interests, and hopes much like our own. A delegation consisting of the mayor of Simferopol, the university president, and an interpreter were due to arrive in Salem in about a week, and we were concerned that we hadn't done much publicity. Then an amazing thing happened. The congressman representing Oregon's Fifth Congressional District, which includes Salem, asked President Reagan to retract the delegation's visas because he didn't like the thought of communists visiting his hometown. President Reagan refused, and the local paper got wind of the controversy and ran front-page headlines for six consecutive days. By the time the delegation arrived in Salem, people were lining the streets, cheering and waving Ukrainian and American flags. City hall had a reception for our guests the likes of which has never been seen before or since. Bands played, school children from the Old Believers community in Gervais sang Russian folk songs, and dignitaries welcomed our guests and presented them with a key to the city. It was a celebration that far exceeded the expectations of our planning committee, and it led to a dynamic and productive exchange program between our two cities, including students, teachers, soccer teams, mountaineers, musicians, vintners, and many other groups. It was a bright moment in the dark and bellicose days of the Cold War, and the success seemed like a minor miracle. About 160 U.S.-Soviet sister city parings occurred through citizen-to-citizen diplomacy. We may never know how much these efforts contributed to détente between our two countries, but it seemed to thaw the hostile rhetoric between Presidents Reagan and Gorbachev.

Have you known people who look for the best in nearly every situation? Their positive and expectant attitude can be infectious. I think God is like that, and every once in a while God finds a way to simply sweep us off our feet. I was attending a conference in Assisi, Italy in 2012, and had taken advantage of some free time to visit a church, the Porziuncola. While resting quietly in a stall, about forty Franciscan friars quickly entered the small sanctuary, fell to their knees, and began to pray in unison. At first I felt I should discretely leave their space, but then I relaxed and allowed the prayers to wash over me like a cleansing shower or perhaps a baptism. Then the monks rose and sang in unison, and I felt all the more blessed and filled with gratitude. Without warning and just as suddenly, they were gone, like it all had been a dream. How extraordinary! I had been touched by the Spirit in a deep and personal way, and it was pure grace.

None of us are experts in spirituality; we are just seekers trying to figure out how to get closer to God's universal spirit of love and compassion. When we first try to pray, we will not be polished and may stumble and fumble our words. But God doesn't mind and is delighted at our attempt; it's our intent, not our eloquence, that matters. Sometimes we may want to borrow the words of someone more experienced, such as Francis of Assisi (1181–1226). Francis came from a well-to-do family whose father was a silk merchant. Yet like Paul and many others, he came to understand, "Who I am is who I am in God." Nothing else mattered by comparison, least of all material comforts or a lifestyle of privilege and affluence. Here is the prayer that bears his name:

> Lord, make me an instrument of your peace:
> where there is hatred, let me sow love;
> where there is injury, pardon;
> where there is doubt, faith;
> where there is despair, hope;
> where there is darkness, light;
> where there is sadness, joy.
>
> O divine Master, grant that I may not so much seek
> to be consoled as to console,
> to be understood as to understand,
> to be loved as to love.
> For it is in giving that we receive.
> It is in pardoning that we are pardoned,
> and it is in dying that we are born to eternal life.
> Amen.

CHAPTER 17

Our Spiritual Journey Forward

EACH OF US IS a unique expression of the divine creation. So too we experience God in different and unique ways. There is no one "self-help" path that assures us a close encounter with the Almighty. We can learn from others, but their journey is not our journey. All the spiritual books in the world simply tell us about other people's experience of God. While we may admire and learn from Francis of Assisi, Thomas Merton, and Mother Theresa, our experience of God will be different, at times inspiring and at times frustrating. We must follow our own unique path, trusting God to show us the way. God is seeking a close relationship with each of us, and the arms of God are big enough to embrace us all.

God is far beyond our comprehension, and each of us is sensing just a fragment of God through our faith. Our calling is to nurture the ray of light, the small insight with which we have been gifted. That is enough to build a profound faith and trust in God. We are all at different stages of our spiritual journey; some are just getting started and some have progressed to a place of deep spirituality. God loves and values each of us wherever we are on our path.

The criminal on the cross at Jesus' crucifixion said, "Jesus, remember me when you come into your kingdom," and Jesus replied, "I tell you the truth, today you will be with me in paradise" (Luke 23:43). All are welcome into the kingdom of heaven, whenever we seek

God and make a commitment. Jesus told the following parable to illustrate that it is never too late:

> For the kingdom of heaven is like a landowner who went out early in the morning to hire men to work in his vineyard. He agreed to pay them a denarius for the day and sent them into his vineyard.
>
> About the third hour he went out and saw others standing in the marketplace doing nothing. He told them, "You also go and work in my vineyard, and I will pay you whatever is right." So they went.
>
> He went out again about the sixth hour and the ninth hour and did the same thing. About the eleventh hour he went out and found still others standing around. He asked them, "Why have you been standing here all day long doing nothing?" "Because no one has hired us," they answered. He said to them, "You also go and work in my vineyard."
>
> When evening came, the owner of the vineyard said to his foreman, "Call the workers and pay them their wages, beginning with the last ones hired and going on to the first."
>
> The workers who were hired about the eleventh hour came and each received a denarius. So when those came who were hired first, they expected to receive more. But each one of them also received a denarius. When they received it, they began to grumble against the landowner.
>
> "These men who were hired last worked only one hour," they said, "and you have made them equal to us who have borne the burden of the work and the heat of the day."
>
> But he answered one of them, "Friend, I am not being unfair to you. Didn't you agree to work for a denarius? Take your pay and go. I want to give the man who was hired last the same as I gave you. Don't I have the right to do what I want with my own money? Or are you envious because I am generous?
>
> So the last will be first, and the first will be last.

(Matthew 20:1–16)

What a remarkable parable! Jesus knew how to upend our preconceived notions of fairness and worthiness. All of us who are workers in God's vineyard will be rewarded with salvation, no matter when we sign on.

We should appreciate and encourage each person's spiritual journey and be grateful for the unique gifts each brings to the table. Paul writes, "There are different kinds of gifts, but the same Spirit distributes them. There are different kinds of service, but the same Lord . . . Now to each one the manifestation of the Spirit is given for the common good" (1 Corinthians 12:4–7). While we each bring unique talents for God's kingdom on Earth, Paul goes on to say that we are all part of the same fellowship of believers: "The body is a unit, though it is made up of many parts; and though all its parts are many, they form one body . . . (T)hose parts of the body that seem to be weaker are indispensable." (1 Corinthians 12:12, 22). All of us can be used for God's purposes, whatever our abilities or limitations.

We are all invited to share in the abundance of God's love, a life-changing experience that provides new purpose and meaning for our lives. Thomas Keating writes, "We too must love not in order to become something, but because we are called to be stewards of divine love; to be identified with it and to be channels for this immense energy, till the world is transformed by Christ and he is all in all."[1]

I recognize that God is unknowable, and that is just fine by me. All I want is to brush lightly against the immense goodness of God's love; the tiniest morsel of God's feast is more than enough. Our aim should be to sense God's presence as often as possible. At times, we may feel flooded with God's grace and love, especially when we are most in need and feeling overwhelmed. More often we may feel just a trickle of God's love and compassion, or we may feel that God is absent altogether. But glimmers of the Almighty can be enough to renew our spirit and carry us forward on our spiritual journey.

1. Keating, Daily Reader, 333.

What becomes evident as we get older, and perhaps wiser, is that life is about more than accomplishments and performance. It is not so much about acting smart, saying the right things, and gaining the respect of our peers. Somewhere in our DNA we have a yearning for something more than the superficialities and busyness that tend to dominate our lives. We may not recognize it, but we long for a deep and vital connection to God, where we can touch the wellspring of divine love. Counselor and author Brent Curtis wrote, "This longing is the most powerful part of any human personality. It fuels our search for meaning, for wholeness, for a sense of being truly alive. However we may describe this deep desire, it is the most important thing about us, our heart of hearts, the passion of our life. And the voice that calls to us in this place is none other than the voice of God."[2]

The good news is that God offers us intimacy, passion, and a new life. Coming nearer to the heart of God allows us to live our lives from a place of God's abundance. By choosing to open ourselves to God's presence through prayer and meditation, we are forgiven, healed, and renewed with God's love. Once this becomes part of our routine practice, we don't want to live without it, because we know we are recipients of God's grace. If we keep at it daily, say for a month, we will not be disappointed. God is seeking this connection with each of us and will take the opportunity to enfold us with love and compassion. We will have a sense of peace, acceptance, and gratitude. God's presence comes as a gift, freely given and wholly undeserved. It may come as the merest hint, like the scent of roses wafting from a neighbor's garden. At other times God's spirit may fill our being, and we will feel transformed and at one with the divine spirit.

Fortunately we don't have to be a mystic, or saint, or member of any particular denomination or congregation to have this experience; it is open to all who seek to connect with God. Everyone can feel renewed and blessed by coming close to God's holiness. Mysteriously we find that we want to reach out to others with love and compassion, and help bring hope to a hurting world. "Ask and it will be given to you; seek and you will find; knock and the door will be

2. Curtis, *Sacred Romance*, 7.

opened to you. For everyone who asks receives; he who seeks finds; and to him who knocks, the door will be opened" (John 11:9–10).

In this epic battle between good and evil, we should not remain as spectators on the sidelines. Jesus told his followers to "be as shrewd as snakes and as innocent as doves" (Matthew 10:16). Jesus defied the power and authority of Jewish leaders and was outspoken about the hypocrisy and hard-heartedness of the Pharisees. He engaged in civil disobedience when he overturned the tables of those selling sacrifices and changing money in the temple (Mark 11:15–16). At the Last Supper he instructed his disciples to serve in his name with everything they have (Luke 22:30).

This is no time for complacency; to the contrary, we are to be fully engaged in God's calling for peace and justice. When we say, "Thy kingdom come, thy will be done," our prayer is more than wishful thinking; we are partnering to make God's kingdom a reality. Jesus taught that God favors the outcast, the poor, the weak, the hungry, and the persecuted, and he modeled how to be outspoken and engaged in social justice. There is enough bread to go around for all people if we learn to share and include everyone at the table. As recipients of God's blessings, we feel compelled to welcome the stranger, to reach out to the lonely, to feed the hungry, to clothe the poor, to take care of the sick, to visit those in prison, and to love our enemy.

As an analogy, we might think of ourselves as part of a symphony orchestra, playing an opus titled "Life." Sometimes the score is heroic, sometimes tragic, occasionally gentle and melodic. What is so very clear is that we are *not* the conductor of the orchestra. We have never rehearsed the score. We don't even know how many movements there will be, much less how the symphony is going to end. To play in the orchestra takes trust, complete trust in the Creator and Conductor, and working together in harmony with the other musicians. Our role is to be attuned, present, watchful, expectantly waiting for our part, whether it is minuscule or major.

We are at a critical point in time, as Susan Hendershot writes: "We need to come back into a right relationship with the sacred, with one another, and with the earth . . . We can no longer live as if humans are the center, but we must recover our sense of the interconnectedness of all things on the planet. It's not only our physical existence that is at stake, but our spiritual existence as well."[3] Faced with our own self-centered habits, and stuck with a polarized, largely dysfunctional national government, we humans are failing miserably to solve the major issues of our day. Our hope is to seek a partnership with the Almighty, where all things are possible. In the words of the prophet Jeremiah, "For surely I know the plans I have for you, says the Lord, plans for your welfare and not for harm, to give you a future with hope" (Jeremiah 29:11). Ultimately, hope for ourselves and for humanity is our spiritual connection to God. The necessary actions we need to take will be more evident through our faith. God plants a spiritual seed in each of us, and we need to nurture that seed. As we have been blessed, we are to be a blessing and encouragement to others, to help them pursue their own unique faith journeys. Our individual and collective spiritual transformation is the way forward in these dark and uncertain times.

When Jesus said, "You are the light of the world" (Matthew 5:13), he was talking about us. How remarkable it is that we are to shine God's reflected light into the dark corners of this world! We are called to share in God's transforming love, to be a resource of justice and hope, and to be active participants in God's redemption of the world. We will find that God can do amazing things with our lives and talents, giving us the strength, wisdom, and love to carry out God's purpose.

3. Hendershot, Interfaith Power and Light email, August 29, 2019.

Epilogue

Spirituality & Social Action was in the hands of the typesetter as the scourge of COVID-19 insidiously traveled around the world. How such a tiny organism, about 120 nanometers in diameter (one thousandth the width of human hair), can create such havoc is extraordinary and frightening. The pandemic has yet to peak, but I worry most about some of the poorest parts of the world, e.g. India and Africa, where clean water is scarce, social distancing is rarely an option, and good hygiene is a challenge even in the best of times. As we have seen in other instances, people who are poor, sick and marginalized are at greatest risk of contracting disease. While this is especially true in low-income countries, it is also a reality among the homeless, living on the streets or crowded into shelters in America. Disasters simply magnify economic disparity and reveal gaping holes in our social safety net.

At this time when many people are out of work, restaurants are closed, and sports and entertainment are canceled, life has come to a grinding halt for those who are not providing essential services. Many governors have ordered us to shelter-in-place, venturing outside only for groceries, medications and some exercise. As we hunker down with few of our customary distractions, the relative quiet and isolation of our homes may open a space for individual growth. Consider this an opportunity to seek the heart of God through prayer, meditation and reflection.

Even in these challenging days, we have much for which to be thankful, including the healthcare workers who are on the front lines of the infection (doctors, nurses, paramedics, aides, orderlies, hospital cleaning staff, morticians, etc.), manufacturers of ventilators, masks, gowns and other equipment; the farmers, grocers and delivery people who provide food for our table; the scientists who are working around the clock to test treatments and to discover a vaccine; and all the many other providers of essential services. Many of them risk their own lives, and we are truly grateful for these heroes, as we could not survive without them.

Even though we are less than three weeks into the shelter-in-place order of our governor, it has become apparent that while we need to practice social distancing, we must not underestimate the innate human need for companionship and touch. We must advocate for public health safety while allowing some degree of socialization. Can we find ways to minister to those who are lonely, elderly, sick and isolated? We need to be cautious when we turn our personal freedoms, our businesses, and our livelihoods over to the dictates of political leaders, since some politicians may abuse this power. If we live with perpetual fear and the sense that we are waging constant war, then we are not living in tune with God's providence.

At times of sorrow and disaster humans have a remarkable capacity to transform fear into compassion and courage. Even as we keep a safe distance from others, we can volunteer to deliver Meals on Wheels, we can prepare meals for the homeless at a soup kitchen, and we can help stock food banks with goods donated by grocery outlets and generous citizens. We can even talk to the unsheltered person living under a bridge to find out about his/her immediate needs, standing at a respectful distance to not compromise our own health. Our capacity for fear is great but so is our capacity for love.

In times of crisis people often ask deep and thought-provoking questions: Why is this happening to us? Is there a God, and if so, why does God allow such suffering? How do we cope with hardships and be courageous at the same time? What risks can we take for the common good without unnecessarily endangering ourselves? Why didn't we tackle the injustice of economic disparity before it became a full-blown crisis? What could be our role to mitigate the climate crisis? Will we work for racial, ethnic, and religious justice, embracing all people, and loving our Black, Hispanic, Muslim, Jewish, and LGBTQ brothers and sisters?

We are being forced to ask tough questions, and that is always the first step in transformation. We have never felt so connected to others around the world, because we all face a common threat. We will get through this, and my guess is we will feel more like a global community, and be more compassionate people when we come out the other side. Let us make room for the sacred to guide us in all our encounters and decisions. God is the priceless ingredient, allowing us to move forward with compassion, love and hope.

After we peel back the layers of ego, busyness and materialism, we discover that at our core we are indeed spiritual beings. How remarkable that God has been with us all along, but we were too distracted or chose not to notice. Someone has said, "Change is constant; growth is optional," and the present is no better time for growth. Suffering is part of the package of life, but suffering will not have the last word. We are not alone, and only God has the last word.

Bibliography

Alexander, Michelle. *The New Jim Crow*. New York: New Press, 2010.

Bell, Rob. *Velvet Elvis: Repainting the Christian Faith*. Grand Rapids: Zondervan, 2005.

Blakemore, Erin. "How the GI Bill's Promise Was Denied to a Million Black WWII Veterans." *History.com*, September 30, 2019. https://www.history.com/news/gi-bill-black-wwii-veterans-benefits.

Borg, Marcus. *The Heart of Christianity: Rediscovering a Life of Faith*. New York: HarperCollins, 2003.

Brown, Brené. *Braving the Wilderness: The Quest for True Belonging and the Courage to Stand Alone*. New York: Random House, 2017.

———. *Gifts of Imperfection: Let Go of Who You Think You're Supposed to Be and Embrace Who You Are*. Center City, MN: Hazelden, 2010.

Brueggemann, Walter. *Journey to the Common Good*. Louisville: Westminster John Knox, 2010.

Chardin, Pierre Teilhard de. *The Heart of Matter*. New York: Harcourt Brace, 1976.

Claiborne, Shane, and John M. Perkins. *Follow Me to Freedom: Leading and Following as an Ordinary Radical*. Ventura, CA: Regal, 2009.

Coffin, William Sloane. *A Passion for the Possible*. Louisville: Westminster John Knox, 1993.

———. *Credo*. Louisville: Westminster John Knox, 2004.

Curtis, Brent, and John Eldredge. *The Sacred Romance: Drawing Closer to the Heart of God*. Nashville: Nelson, 1997.

Dozier, Verna. *The Dream of God: A Call to Return*. Cambridge: Cowley, 1991.

Drummond, Henry. *The Greatest Thing in the World and Other Addresses*. New York: G & D Media, 2019.

Francis, Pope. "Evangelii Gaudium." Apostolic exhortation, November 24, 2013. http://www.vatican.va/content/francesco/en/apost_exhortations/documents/papa-francesco_esortazione-ap_20131124_evangelii-gaudium.html.

Gutenson, Charles E. *Christians and the Common Good: How Faith Intersects with Public Life*. Grand Rapids: Brazos, 2011.

Hawken, Paul. *Blessed Unrest: How the Largest Movement in the World Came into Being and Why No One Saw It Coming.* New York: Viking, 2007.

Heschel, Abraham Joshua. *God in Search of Man.* New York: Farrar, Straus & Giroux, 1976.

Hill, Daniel. *White Awake: An Honest Look at What It Means to Be White.* Downers Grove, IL: InterVarsity, 2017.

Ingraham, Christopher. "Not Only Are Americans Becoming Less Happy— We're Experiencing More Pain Too." *Washington Post*, December 6, 2017. https://www.washingtonpost.com/news/wonk/wp/2017/12/06/not-only-are-americans-becoming-less-happy-were-experiencing-more-pain-too/.

Institute on Taxation and Economic Policy. *Corporate Tax Avoidance Remains Rampant Under New Tax Law.* April 11, 2019. https://itep.org/notadime/

Keating, Thomas. *Intimacy with God: An Introduction to Centering Prayer.* New York: Crossroad, 2004.

———. *Open Mind, Open Heart: The Contemplative Dimension of the Gospel.* Petaling Jaya: Arrupe, 2001.

———. *The Daily Reader for Contemplative Living.* New York: Continuum, 2005.

———. *The Heart of the World: An Introduction to Contemplative Christianity.* New York: Crossroad, 2008.

King, Martin Luther, Jr. *I Have a Dream: Writings and Speeches That Changed the World.* New York: HarperCollins, 1992.

———. *Strength to Love.* Philadelphia: Fortress, 1981.

Kolodiejchuk, Brian, editor. *Mother Teresa: Come Be My Light: The Private Writings of the "Saint of Calcutta."* New York: Doubleday, 2007.

Kornfield, Jack. *A Path with Heart: A Guide through the Perils and Promises of Spiritual Life.* New York: Bantam, 1993.

Lakey, George. *How We Win: A Guide to Nonviolent Direct Action Campaigning.* Brooklyn, NY: Melville House, 2018.

Leopold, Les. *Runaway Inequality: An Activist's Guide to Economic Justice.* New York: Labor Institute, 2018.

Lepore, Jill. *This America: The Case for the Nation.* New York: Liverwright, 2019.

Lewis, C. S. *Mere Christianity.* New York: HarperCollins, 2001.

———. *The Joyful Christian.* New York: Touchstone, 1977.

Lucado, Max. *Unshakable Hope: Building Our Lives on the Promises of God.* Nashville: Nelson, 2018.

Manning, Brennan. *All Is Grace.* Colorado Springs: Cook, 2011.

———. *Lion and Lamb: The Relentless Tenderness of Jesus.* Tarrytown, NY: Chosen, 1986.

———. *The Ragamuffin Gospel.* Colorado Springs: Multnomah, 2015.

———. *Ruthless Trust: The Ragamuffin's Path to God.* New York: HarperCollins, 2000.

Mattson, Stephen. *The Great Reckoning: Surviving a Christianity That Looks Nothing Like Christ.* Harrisonburg, VA: Herald, 2018.

———. "Pursuing Justice As an Act of Worship." *Sojourners*, January 16, 2019. https://sojo.net/articles/pursuing-justice-act-worship.

McLaren, Brian D. *The Great Spiritual Migration: How the World's Largest Religion Is Seeking a Better Way to Be Christian.* New York: Convergent, 2016.

———. *Why Did Jesus, Moses, the Buddha, and Mohammed Cross the Road?: Christian Identity in a Multi-Faith World.* New York: Jericho, 2013.

Merton, Thomas. *Choosing to Love the World.* Boulder, CO: Sounds True, 2008.

Myers, Ched. *Binding the Strong Man: A Political Reading of Mark's Story of Jesus.* New York: Maryknoll, 2008.

———. "Nature against Empire: Exodus Plagues, Climate Crisis and Hardheartedness." *Watershed Discipleship*, 2018. https://watersheddiscipleship.org.

———. *Watershed Discipleship: Reinhabiting Bioregional Faith and Practice.* Eugene, OR: Wipf & Stock, 2016.

———. *Who Will Roll Away the Stone?: Discipleship Queries for First World Christians.* Maryknoll, NY: Orbis, 1994.

Nouwen, Henri. *Making All Things New: An Invitation to the Spiritual Life.* San Francisco: Harper & Row, 1981.

O'Connor, Elizabeth. *Cry Pain, Cry Hope: A Guide to the Dimensions of Call.* Washington, DC: Potter's House, 2002.

Olsen, Jared, "We Should End Federal Executions." *New York Times*, July 31, 2019.

Rohr's Daily Meditation, *Substitutionary Atonement*, 7/22/17

Rohr's Daily Meditation, *A Nonviolent Atonement*, 7/24/17

Rohr, Richard. *Contemplation in Action.* New York: Crossroad, 2006.

———. *Falling Upward: A Spirituality for the Two Halves of Life.* San Francisco: Jossey-Bass, 2011.

———. *Hope Against Darkness: The Transforming Vision of Saint Francis in an Age of Anxiety.* Cincinnati: St. Anthony Messenger, 2001.

———. *Immortal Diamond: The Search for Our True Self.* San Francisco: Jossey-Bass, 2013.

———. *Just This.* Albuquerque: CAC, 2017.

———. *The Naked Now: Learning to See as the Mystics See.* New York: Crossroad, 2009.

———. *Things Hidden: Scripture as Spirituality.* Cincinnati: St. Anthony Messenger, 2008.

Sider, Ronald J. *Just Generosity: A New Vision for Overcoming Poverty in America.* Grand Rapids: Baker, 2007.

———. *Rich Christians in an Age of Hunger: Moving from Affluence to Generosity.* Nashville: Word, 1997.

———. *The Scandal of the Evangelical Conscience: Why Are Christians Living Just Like the Rest of the World?* Ada, MI: Baker, 2005.

Stumbo, John, and Joanna Stumbo. *An Honest Look at a Mysterious Journey.* Fox Island, WA: Nesting Tree, 2011.

Thich Nhat Hanh. *Essential Writings*. Maryknoll, NY: Orbis, 2001.

Tolle, Eckhart. *A New Earth: Awakening to Your Life's Purpose*. London: Penguin, 2005.

Tutu, Desmond. *God Has a Dream: A Vision of Hope for Our Time*. New York: Doubleday, 2004.

Vanier, Jean. *Community and Growth: Our Pilgrimage Together*. New York: Paulist, 1989.

Wallis, Jim. *America's Original Sin: Racism, White Privilege and the Bridge to a New America*. Grand Rapids: Brazos, 2016.

———. *Faith Works: Lessons from the Life of an Activist Preacher*. New York: Random House, 2000.

———. *God's Politics: Why the Right Gets It Wrong and the Left Doesn't Get It*. New York: HarperCollins, 2005.

———. *On God's Side: What Religion Forgets and Politics Hasn't Learned About Serving the Common Good*. Grand Rapids: Brazos, 2013.

———. *Rediscovering Values on Wall Street, Main Street, and Your Street: A Moral Compass for the New Economy*. New York: Howard, 2010.

Yancey, Philip. *Prayer: Does It Make Any Difference?* Grand Rapids: Zondervan, 2006.

———. *What's So Amazing About Grace?* Grand Rapids: Zondervan, 1997.

For more information or to contact the author,
please visit the website:

www.SpiritualityandSocialAction.com

Made in the USA
Coppell, TX
16 May 2020